Table Talk

Table Talk

Rethinking Communion and Community

Mike Graves

CASCADE *Books* · Eugene, Oregon

TABLE TALK
Rethinking Communion and Community

Cascade Books
An Imprint of Wipf and Stock Publishers
199 W. 8th Ave., Suite 3
Eugene, OR 97401

www.wipfandstock.com

PAPERBACK ISBN: 978-1-5326-1877-2
HARDCOVER ISBN: 978-1-4982-4458-9
EBOOK ISBN: 978-1-4982-4457-2

Cataloguing-in-Publication data:

Names: Graves, Mike.

Title: Table talk : rethinking communion and community / Mike Graves.

Description: Eugene, OR: Cascade Books, 2017 | Includes bibliographical references.

Identifiers: ISBN 978-1-5326-1877-2 (paperback) | ISBN 978-1-4982-4458-9 (hardcover) | ISBN 978-1-4982-4457-2 (ebook)

Subjects: LCSH: Table—Religious aspects. | Lord's Supper—Biblical Teaching. | Title.

Classification: BV823 .G75 2017 (print) | BV823 (ebook)

Manufactured in the USA   10/20/17

For my mom, Dorothy, who fed me first and taught me to eat;
I miss you, and your oatmeal cookies

And for our young granddaughters, Emma and Olivia;
I can't wait to bake cookies with both of you

"A book about meals is a book about magic—the magical transformation of people into the identities constructed by the foods they ingest, the group they dine with, and the ideas they share at their gatherings."

—SUSAN MARKS

Contents

Food for Thought

- What if I told you that the way Christians worship and eat Communion today is not just 2,000 years removed from the first century but in many ways light years removed, that those earliest followers of Jesus might not even recognize our worship services?

- What if I told you they gathered primarily to eat, and when those earliest house churches started to grow, they made more room by converting the dining room into meeting space and the loss was more catastrophic than we ever could have imagined?

- What if I told you that their Communion meal was more of a festive dinner party, celebrating and enjoying the presence of the resurrected Jesus?

- What if I told you that the first followers of Jesus had extended conversations over wine after dinner, valuing the voices of everyone present, and that conversation was their notion of preaching?

- What if I told you that in conventional church services, new ways of eating Communion are enlivening congregations, giving them reasons to celebrate together in festive joy?

- What if I told you that a new movement of God is afoot in our day, a movement called dinner church at which people gather around a meal and have a conversation as they remember Jesus and celebrate their part in God's family?

An Invitation

"Persons matter at the table. We sit in real and estimable places marked with the most precious and intimate device we have: our names."

—Robert Farrar Capon

Table Talk

I think it's fair to say Luna Azteca tops the list of our family's favorite Mexican restaurants in the Kansas City area. The pork carnitas never cease to amaze me, tender as pot roast and oh so good on a fresh flour tortilla with some guacamole, shredded cheese, maybe some onions. My wife loves their tamales and would add salsa verde too, the "green stuff." We probably average eating there three times a month, especially on Taco Tuesday. But I'm thinking here about a meal we had one Friday, out on the patio there, ten of us in all. My wife and I, our three grown children and their significant others, as well as another couple, gathered there on a beautiful evening late in the summer of 2014.

The chips and salsa were disappearing as the drinks began appearing. This was an occasion because our oldest and his wife moved to Orlando years ago now, but she was in town to see her sister's new baby and our son was in town on business. We usually get to see them only at Christmas, maybe one other time of the year, so this was a bonus visit.

Everyone ordered and we feasted. Several had the carnitas, others the chipotle enchiladas, and some the tacos. Near the end of dinner our daughter-in-law fetched a present out of her purse and put it down in front of my wife. I leaned in, curious. Our anniversary had already passed and neither of us had a birthday upcoming, so we were a bit stumped. The present turned out to be about someone else's birthday, an upcoming birth. We were going to be grandparents, our first grandchild. Seven months later Emma Faye Graves came into the world, but on that Friday at Luna Azteca we were already in love with her.

Even if the details are markedly different, I'm guessing you can relate to the story, recalling a special meal with friends and family, when the food and drinks tasted better than ever because of the occasion. Maybe someone announced an engagement, told about a promotion, or shared about a lump that turned out to be benign. There is something special about sharing life over a meal with people you love. While it might not seem like it, this sort of sharing over dinner is closer than you might imagine to what those earliest followers of Jesus did when they gathered together. Not exactly, of course, because all analogies break down. But it's closer than you might think because it was around a table they shared their lives as Christians.

Mark it down, other than our beds the table is the most intimate piece of furniture in our lives. The bed is obvious enough, the place where in the dark of night we make ourselves vulnerable as we give into sleep and dreams, the place where we make love, make babies. But make no mistake, the table is intimate too. It is at table that we open our mouths to put food in. It is at table we occasionally drop crumbs, wipe our faces, and stifle burps. Oh, the fleshiness and messiness of it all! It is at the table that we share more than bread; we share stories, share our dreams, share our very lives together. In his classic book *For the Life of the World*, Alexander Schmemann writes, "Centuries of secularism have failed to transform eating into something strictly utilitarian. Food is still treated with reverence . . . . To eat is still something more than to maintain bodily functions."[1] Schememann begins that book with a familiar line from the philosopher Ludwig Feuerbach: we are what we eat. If it is true that in many ways we are *what* we eat, it is also true that *how* we eat says much about us. In other words, show us how people eat and we will learn more about them than we might have imagined. This is a book about how we eat, not as humans in general, carnivores versus vegetarians, that sort of thing. Nor is it more narrowly about how we eat as Americans pulling up to a drive-thru window, scarfing down burgers and fries on the way to our kid's dance recital or soccer game, although a different pace of church life could speak to these things.[2] This book is about how we eat as church gathered in worship.

* * *

AN INVITATION

I suppose it would be easy to read this quote by Andrew McGowan about those earliest followers of Jesus while stifling a yawn: "Christians met for meals."[3] It hardly seems a striking observation. Except when you stop to think about it, this is startling news indeed, that when those first followers of Jesus got together for what we now call "worship" or "church," they did so to eat. They didn't file into rows of wooden pews or folding chairs to sit still and listen to a sermon, or a choir, or any of the things we might conjure in our minds today. McGowan's insight is truly profound: "Christians met for meals." Today congregations might gather for a social meal in the fellowship hall every once in a while, but this was their normal way of gathering, and the main reason. After dinner they had conversations over wine on a host of topics, including stories about their daily lives as well as stories about Jesus. In other words, a time at the table followed by a talk, which sounds like two things, except the talking took place at table too. Table talk.[4] Today it is common for Christians to gather for a talk called sermon and a meal called Communion, but oh how things have changed.

This book looks at those early meals that Jesus' followers ate, seeking answers to a host of questions: what exactly was an "upper room"? We hear that term tossed about, but what does it mean? Was there only one or was this a typical dwelling? Who was invited to these dinner gatherings? How many people were typically present? Besides bread and wine, what did our ancestors in the faith eat? How was their eating different from others in the Mediterranean world? How was it the same? How exactly did they gather together? But the questions we will explore are not just rooted in the past because ultimately we will want to think about what their dining practices might say about the way we eat and gather as church now.

* * *

One Christmas break when our grown children were home for the holidays, they spent their time doing all the usual stuff: napping, playing video games, reading, watching movies, cooking, just hanging out. Whenever I could find the time, I spent my holidays reading books about ancient Greco-Roman banqueting, the kinds of meals that those earliest followers of Jesus inherited and that greatly impacted how they ate a meal in Jesus' name. Every once in a while I would exclaim, "Oh, my God, this is *so* interesting. Listen to this." They would pause whatever it was they were doing, and I would share some insight, only to be met with puzzled looks. They were not impressed with my findings, suspecting their dad was some sort of nerd.

3

To such a charge I plead innocent, my evidence coming in the form of another story. After our granddaughter Emma was born, we naturally made several trips to Orlando, including one fall while I was on sabbatical working on this book. One afternoon I went out to play some golf and got paired up with a couple of fellows I didn't know, Bob and Les. About thirty minutes into the round the small talk turned to what we do for a living.

"Yeah, we're both retired now. What about you?"

"Me, I'm a seminary professor in Kansas City. I teach people preparing for ministry."

"Really? Les and I go to a church not far from here. Seminary professor, that's so cool."

(This is not the essence of my defense, that they thought I was cool. The conversation continued.)

"So how come you're not back in Kansas City teaching?"

"Oh, I'm on a research leave, working on a book about how the earliest followers of Jesus ate together and what that might mean when churches eat in remembrance of him now."

"How churches eat, huh? You mean Communion?"

"I was just going to ask you what you call it at your church since different Christian traditions use different names."

"Yeah, we call it Communion. Although we don't do it very often, every couple of months, something like that."

"And when you do, what's it like? How would you describe it?"

Bob thought for a moment. "How would I describe it?" Clearly the question had never occurred to him before. He looked at his buddy, both shrugging their shoulders. He said, "I don't know, a holy time. A quiet time."

Long pause.

Les chimed in, "Kind of like a funeral. Well, not exactly, but you get the idea. Respectful. Serious."

I told them that sounded familiar, and then shared an insight that blew my mind when I first discovered it and still does. I said, "The meals of those first followers of Jesus were not the least bit like funerals, more like festive dinner parties." That's when one of my new golf buddies in Florida said, "My God, that would be amazing. I can't quite picture it, but a festive dinner party as church. That would be different." They mumbled about that the rest of the round.

This one insight forms the core of this book, the church's eating as a joyful gathering, a kind of dinner party. As we will see, except for Holy

Week when believers focused on the death of Jesus, the rest of the time their eating together was mostly festive. Two thousand years later the meal we eat when gathered as church is frequently anything but joyful, more like a funeral than a feast. It's as if we have forgotten that Jesus has been raised from the dead, that he is present with us now in the gathered community, and that he promises to eat with us upon his return. Those are all wonderful reasons for feasting. So let me repeat: their evening meals were festive dinner parties.

This book is the story of that meal—not down through the ages as theologians arm-wrestled over its meaning (Is Jesus really present in the elements? What happens to the bread and wine when an ordained person prays over them? What might happen to us if we eat it wrongly?); and not about denominational squabbles (Can young children participate? What if I'm not a member of that church? What if I'm not baptized or in good standing?). Those are later levels in the exploration of the Jesus meal worth considering, but that's not where my interest lies, even if I might touch on some related topics along the way.

* * *

It would be misleading to say I grew up in church, but I was drug there enough Sundays—and have seen enough families with children in tow over the years since then—to recognize two rules parents regularly enforce: we don't talk in church and we certainly don't eat in church. Surely you recognize those rules. The first liturgical lesson of childhood comes from an adult shushing us. And the idea of bringing food into the church? Forget it. We don't eat and talk in church. But those are rules I would like for us to rethink as we reflect on our present Communion practices, especially at a time like this .

Here's what I mean. Religion writer Phyllis Tickle claims that every 500 years or so the church hosts a giant rummage sale and makes wholesale changes. If the math is correct, half a millennium after the Protestant Reformation of 1517 is an ideal time for one such change, namely rethinking how the church eats when gathered. For those who don't know, October 31 marks the anniversary of Martin Luther nailing his list of ninety-five complaints to a door in Wittenberg, Germany.[5] To be clear, I have no plans to nail copies of this book on any church's door, but I am hopeful that Christians of all persuasions might rethink the Jesus meal.

This present exploration, then, is rooted primarily in two different eras: the first century when the Jesus movement was just beginning, and the present. Having skipped over two millennia of history and theology, please be assured I have no naïve notions of reclaiming their ancient practices wholesale, copying everything they did. Back then they wore tunics and sandals, too, which might have been fun when I was in college, but no thanks. They also had no private bathrooms, relieving themselves in public, or in a bathhouse without stalls. Again, no thanks. And it's not like everything those earliest followers did turned to gold, not hardly. We have a tendency to romanticize when it comes to those earliest followers of Jesus. They had problems, even at the table. If they hadn't, we might not know as much as we do about their eating together.

There are certain practices, however, that our first ancestors in the faith followed, practices that have been lost to us that we might reclaim, especially when it comes to eating joyfully as a church. You've heard the expression, how folks did church "back in the 50s." That's something of the idea, only not the 1950s but the 50s. What might that look like today? Here's my hunch: if we could travel back to those earliest Christian gatherings, we would realize we are not just 2,000 years removed; we are light years removed from how they ate when gathered. In particular, four characteristics of their Communion practices would leap out at us, traits that are scattered throughout the New Testament, but that often go unnoticed.

In the first place the meal Jesus' followers ate was just that, a full meal as part of a full evening with others. The point is not how many calories they consumed compared to the little crackers or wafers we nibble on in church (although I do find that problematic and will have more to say about this), but the crucial aspect is *the intimacy that naturally developed as they spent a whole evening together eating and talking.* Dinner parties were the norm then and they still are in our day, the kind of gatherings that connect people. We just don't think of the church as a dinner party the way they did. Even when we do eat a meal at church nowadays, we have social halls that are completely separate from our sanctuaries. Eating together is a religious act of sharing our food, our time, our very lives. In chapter one we will look more closely at their meal practices and ours.

Second, unlike many banqueting groups back then, these Christian feasts were *mostly inclusive,* breaking down barriers of gender and socio-economic status. Theirs weren't the only dinner parties that practiced inclusion, nor were they always consistent in that practice (thus, the qualifier *mostly*); but it did become a hallmark of their eating as followers of Jesus. Today most churches invite everyone present to join them after worship for a potluck supper because hospitality is part of what it means to be Christian, especially with food; it's in our DNA as followers of Jesus to be welcoming. Gathering around a table is the perfect place for welcoming others. Unfortunately, when it comes to the meal in the sanctuary, that is often an exclusive affair, certain persons not welcome at this one table, and for a variety of reasons. Chapter two considers the justice implications of the church's eating habits.

Third, as I've already noted, *festive joy* characterized these dinner parties as they enjoyed food and drink, as well as each other's company. In modern terms, no one signaled for the organist to play something somber or for the lights to be lowered while they lowered their heads and spirits. Obviously they didn't have pipe organs to play, but even if they did, such a mood would have made no sense at all. Theirs was a dinner party among friends in the name of the resurrected Christ. Of course life is not always sunny, and so we will want to think about what a festive meal means during times of suffering and anxiety. In our homes we not only share joys around tables but sorrows too. How should we eat when instead of announcing an engagement, friends are splitting up? How does the church eat joyfully in the face of wars around the world and mass shootings on our own soil? What does a festive dinner party in Jesus' name really look like? We will wrestle with these questions and more in chapter three.

Lastly, after dinner everyone *participated in lively conversations* over wine, the key being not how much alcohol was consumed but how everyone could *participate* in the dialogue. In the wider culture there were all sorts of topics citizens might discuss, including which came first, the chicken or the egg, or how many angels can dance on the head of a pin. I'm not making this up. As those first followers of Jesus adapted this pattern from the culture, their table talk was a dialogical sharing of life together with each person having opportunity to participate. Over the centuries these conversations became what we now think of as sermons, talks that worshipers didn't so much participate in but listened to. Even if the word *sermon* is Latin for "talk," most of us don't think of Sunday sermons as after-dinner conversations with give-and-take. But participation by all was extremely important to our ancestors in the faith. Chapter four calls us to rethink preaching in light of their practices and our changing world.

Honestly, the overlap of ancient banqueting practices and how those first Jesus followers ate their meals is in some ways just part of history unfolding. Earlier conquests by Alexander the Great and the resulting Hellenism (or Greek influence), followed by Roman rule in the Mediterranean world overlapping with the birth of the church is pretty much happenstance. Yes, Jesus was a Jew and the Gospel writers go to great lengths to portray the so-called Last Supper as a Passover meal, but even the Passover meal took on the form of a meal and conversation long before Jesus' time.[6]

That said, it's true that I can't find a verse anywhere in the Bible where Jesus or Paul said, "The church is founded on Greco-Roman dinner parties and there are four traits . . . ." No, it's just how people, Jesus included, ate their evening meals when this faith we now call Christianity got started. So in some ways I suppose you could pick any moment in church history, teasing out examples and lessons for us.[7]

But, and this is one really big "but," what took place in those first-century gatherings resonates with the very nature of God and the gospel itself—intimacy, inclusion, festive joy, and participation in community. Many of the historical developments since have led to a loss of these qualities, even as the theology of the meal has become more and more complex. As one scholar notes, many "theologians ask too much of the table in terms of theology and too little of the table in terms of community."[8] Amen to that.

These four traits are also clearly something people crave today, a sense of intimacy and belonging that rarely happens in our churches but is so common among small groups gathered around a meal. The acclaimed food writer Michael Pollan reminds us that we are the only animals that cook our food and take the time to dine; it's what makes us human.[9] The theologian Alexander Schmemann notes that we are the only animals to *bless* God for the food.[10] For those earliest followers of Jesus, eating together and sharing life in Christ was a central piece of what made them Christian.

These four traits, then, serve as an outline of the book's four chapters. But these traits call us to rethink more than just Communion practices; they challenge the very notion of what it means to gather for what we typically call "worship." When I started the research for this book I didn't see this coming, this notion of not just rethinking Communion, but even the way we gather as church. As the scholar Dennis Smith puts it, "The community that began its existence in private homes around a banquet table evolved into a church that met in a meeting hall before an altar."[11]

But that evolution appears to be happening in reverse in some places today. Christian gatherings that have mostly been vertical in proper sanctuaries are becoming more horizontal, more fellowship than worship, and in alternative sites sometimes. For most of the last 2,000 years Christians have oriented themselves toward God while in the presence of others; now a growing number of congregations, part of the dinner church movement, are orienting themselves toward each other in the presence of God. Worship too is something we will want to rethink.

Like those early Christian dinner parties where all were welcome, in these pages you are invited to join me for food and conversation. In fact, instead of simply food for thought, it would suit me just fine if you nibbled on something delicious while reading, maybe a chocolate-filled croissant and a glass of your favorite wine, or a chocolate chip cookie and a glass of milk. Better yet, you could get together with friends over dinner to discuss it. Eating and talking. Table talk. That's how we celebrate Jesus' presence among us, how we remember him.

A Brief Vocabulary Lesson

A few years ago I attended a conference in Nashville, Tennessee. Before catching my flight back home on Sunday afternoon, a colleague and I decided to attend a church nearby we had been told was worth checking out. The person who told us said any church that can get a thousand college students up early every Sunday has something going for it. So my good friend and colleague André and I checked it out. Sure enough, on a chilly December morning the place was packed, although that's not the first thing I noticed.

The first thing anyone could plainly see is the place where this congregation meets is not your typical church building, more of an industrial brick building and with exposed brick walls inside as well. It was a Starbucks church for sure, the kind that lets you bring in a cup of whatever brew you're drinking and provides coffee for anyone present, casual attire the norm.

The architecture was different in another way too, since the whole right side of the place featured a giant bar, and with bottles of beer on display across the back. I thought, *Surely, they don't serve alcohol during church.* No, but the bar *is* where they serve the Lord's Supper. I'm guessing the building still functions as a bar at night, and the church just rents the place.

After the sermon was over, the minister said something to this effect, "Okay, it's time for the Lord's Supper. We have the one big station over on this side." (I'm pretty sure he never used the word *bar*.) He continued, "You can make your way over there, or there are different stations around the room. Get a piece of bread, a little cup of the juice. You can eat it there or bring it back with you, and make your way back to your seat." And that was it. I was in liturgical shock. Not a single word of explanation. No fancy theological language or ancient formulas. No prayers before or after. This was the polar opposite of high church, even lower than low in some ways.

André and I padded over to the bar along with the crowd. There was no one there to serve us or say anything to us; this was self-service, which I'm used to when pumping gas, but the Lord's Supper? Like everyone else, we ate a small bite of incredibly delicious bread, drank from the smallest cup of grape juice ever, and then traipsed back to our seats. The Lord's Supper was over. Shortly thereafter the service was as well. I turned toward André, but he was in conversation with the couple to his left, so I turned to my right and asked the young woman next to me if I could ask her a question about her church. We had introduced ourselves briefly earlier in the service, and she said sure.

I said, "I'm wondering what the Lord's Supper means to you when you eat it here in your church. What do you think about when you take it?" She laughed. Turns out, her boyfriend had asked the same thing when he started attending with her. She said, "Honestly, I didn't know how to answer his question back then. I'm not sure even now. I used to think it was only about confessing my sins, remembering the suffering of Jesus, how he died for my sins." I nodded. She continued, "Then I realized maybe it doesn't always have to be about my sins. So depending on my mood, or where I am in my walk with God, or maybe even what the sermon was about, I might think about those things. Yeah, I guess that's it, but I'm not really sure. What do you think?" I told her I was working on this book, and then added, "To be honest, the meal means a lot of different things, and I don't just mean in terms of personal preference."

Before we go any further there are some terms we need to get clear because the meal we eat in Jesus' name does indeed go by many names: Communion, Lord's Supper, and Eucharist being the most common. Roman Catholics celebrate the Eucharist as part of a service they call the Mass, sometimes even referring to the meal itself as Mass. There's also the lesser-known terms breaking of bread and agape feast. It's likely that one or more of these are part of your own religious heritage, like *Communion* was for my golfing buddy in Florida and *Lord's Supper* for that church in Tennessee. Except here's the tricky part about these different terms. The meal goes by many names not because different denominations laid claim and trademarked them, although there are certain terms preferred by certain churches. No, the meal goes by many names because in many ways the meal means different things in the different passages of Scripture.

Bread and wine are dynamic symbols. The Catholic novelist and writer Andrew Greeley notes how the Bible's beautiful and evocative stories frequently get traded in for doctrinal labels, long Latin or Greek words in particular: "Bethlehem becomes the Incarnation. The empty tomb becomes the Resurrection. The final supper becomes the Eucharist."[12] The writers of the New Testament never capitalize any of the terms we use nowadays, although most of the terms we use come from the New Testament, and most of those from Paul's letters and Luke's two volumes, his Gospel and Acts.

So here's a brief vocabulary lesson. In his first letter to the Corinthians, the earliest written account of this meal, Paul refers to a "sharing" that takes place when believers eat this meal, "The cup of blessing that we bless, is it not a sharing in the blood of Christ? The bread that we break, is it not a sharing in the body of Christ?" (1 Cor 10:16–17). No tradition that I'm aware of refers to the Jesus meal as the Sharing, but the word translated "sharing" is the Greek word *koinonia*, one of a few Greek words some churchgoers have actually heard before. The term can also be translated as fellowship or communion. In other words, there is a communing, or sharing, or fellowshipping with God and each other that takes place in the meal. Capitalized, that's Communion. Some traditions place the qualifier "Holy" in front of Communion, a term meant to imply something special or different about this particular sharing, even if the New Testament doesn't have such qualifiers.

A little later in that same letter Paul refers to "the Lord's supper." He writes, "When you come together, it is not really to eat the Lord's supper. For when the time comes to eat, each of you goes ahead with your own supper, and one goes hungry and another becomes drunk" (1 Cor 11:20–21). Paul contrasts the "*Lord's* supper" with the selfishness they were exhibiting when they ate their "*own* supper" without regard for the poor in the community. Ideally, churches that are observing the "Lord's Supper" (as opposed to their *own*) would be remembering the poorer members of the congregation, and not just the so-called "Last Supper," even if Paul goes on to recall the meal

Jesus ate with his disciples "on the night when he was betrayed" (1 Cor 11:23). We will see later how the Last Supper came to influence the somber Lord's Supper services many of us are familiar with today.

Even the name Eucharist comes from Paul, although I know a lot of Protestants who think some pope dreamed it up or who have never even heard the term before. What a shame since it's such a beautiful word, pronounced *yu-ke-rist*, in case you've not heard it. In that same letter to the church at Corinth, Paul recalls the familiar words of how Jesus "took a loaf of bread, and when he had given thanks, he broke it" (1 Cor 11:23–24). The verb "to give thanks" in that sentence is *eucharistésas* in Greek, Eucharist being the noun form.[13] Celebrating the Eucharist focuses on the meal as an act of thanksgiving.

As for the lesser-known terms, the breaking of bread comes from the writer of the two-volume work Luke-Acts. In one of the early summaries of Acts, the author describes how the followers of Jesus "broke bread at home and ate their food with glad and generous hearts" (Acts 2:46). The breaking of bread is the way Acts will describe this meal we eat in Jesus' name, part of the larger evening meal when they also "ate their food."

Agape feast is likely the least known and least used term, but it is in the New Testament, tucked away in the one-page letter called Jude, which chides the church for the "blemishes" on their "love-feasts" (verse 12). By the third century this feast was at least in some places separated from the Eucharist. But that was a later development since from the start Jesus' followers ate the bread and wine as part of a larger meal gathering, a feasting that could sometimes get out of hand when too much wine was consumed, resulting in too much revelry. We don't usually have that problem nowadays, too much revelry in church.

CHAPTER I

The Meal

"Whatever the Lord's Supper is, it is everything that eating is."

—HOYT HICKMAN

Companions

One of the ways people get to know each other is over a meal, becoming companions (literally, those who break bread together). But since this is a *book* about meals and not a conversation over an *actual* meal, I thought I'd share what brought me to this place of fascination with how we eat in Jesus' name, long before I started reading those scholarly Greco-Roman banqueting books. If you're reading this book with others, this might be the place for each of you to share your own journeys with this meal.

In many ways my journey begins at St. Christopher Catholic Church in Houston, Texas, where I was baptized the fifteenth day of my life and where we attended sporadically at best until I was about nine years old. St. Christopher is considered the patron saint of travelers, so I guess it makes sense that my journey began there, although looking back the road becomes much clearer when I reflect on something that took place more recently, in Oklahoma City.

It was late fall, 1998. At the time, I was teaching at an American Baptist seminary in Kansas City, and had received a flyer promoting one of Robert Webber's workshops on worship. My good friend Ronnie was serving as pastor of a church in Wichita Falls, Texas, and since we had been through PhD work together a few years earlier, Oklahoma City seemed like a good place to meet up for a reunion at Webber's workshop, especially since Ronnie had grown up in one of the suburbs there. A little golf outing, some

Mexican food at a place he knew, and a workshop on worship. What more could a person ask for?

I was familiar with Webber's many volumes on worship, including his slim book *Evangelicals on the Canterbury Trail*, and had used some of them in my classes at the seminary. Still, I honestly didn't have high expectations for the day. I certainly didn't expect it to change my life. Unlike so many scholars in the study of worship, Webber, who has since passed away, could gather up a whole host of denominational traditions to think about worship together. Catholics, Episcopalians, all sorts of mainliners, Evangelicals, they all met to learn from a very gifted and gentle teacher.

The handouts and notes from that day are still around my study somewhere. Webber briefly rehearsed the history of Christian worship, noting how during the Protestant Reformation the church tossed out the Eucharistic baby with the bath water, so to speak. He noted that in reaction to the abuses and even superstitions associated with Holy Communion leading up to that time, instead of repairing the abuses of the Catholic Church, many traditions were born that simply chose not to eat the meal on a regular basis.

Many Christians today are surprised to learn that one of the reasons some denominations only take Communion once a month or so isn't because that makes it more special (a rule never applied to sermons and the offering) but because of an over-reaction to Roman Catholic practice way back in the sixteenth century. Lutherans and Episcopalians, of course, still ate every week, as did Roman Catholics, but for so many traditions, occasional observance ruled the day. A generation later John Calvin may have desired weekly Eucharist, but he was overruled by the Council of Geneva, and so the Church of Scotland and, here in the States, the Presbyterians were out of luck. Something similar would be true for Methodists and John Wesley hundreds of years later.

I listened to Webber and took notes. Like every other person who ever went to seminary, I had studied church history. I didn't remember all the names and dates, although Luther and 1517 stuck out clearly. That Wednesday (I Googled it), October 31, the day Luther supposedly nailed his theses to the door, was the beginning of a new era in the history of the church, even if it wasn't entirely different the next Sunday.

Webber's rehearsal of history was nothing new to me, except somehow it was this particular day. The idea that the church (capital C), or at least a sizable portion of it, had moved away from celebrating the Jesus meal every week hit me hard. It was as if someone had just explained gravity, and suddenly it made sense why what goes up must come down. Only what I felt was the opposite, as if I were no longer tethered to the planet but floating in a new world. How, I wondered, did a large part of Christ's church move from weekly Eucharist to occasional? What were we thinking? I concluded that we weren't thinking, at least not clearly.

Ronnie could tell something was up. He looked at me, eyebrows raised. I looked at him and mouthed, "We're supposed to eat this meal every week." He whispered, "Easy for a seminary professor to say. Not so much for the pastor of a Baptist church." Score one for Ronnie. He was right of course; seminary professors work in ivory towers.

"I'm serious," I told Ronnie. "We're supposed to eat this meal every week. That was the pattern all along."

Still, he was right. Sure, at the time I was preaching every week at Rolling Hills Baptist Church in Fayetteville, Arkansas, but that was as interim minister, not permanent pastor. Ronnie knew he couldn't just announce that from now on the church there in Wichita Falls was returning to that early pattern of weekly Eucharist, or Lord's Supper, as Baptists were fond of calling it. They likely would have associated weekly observance with what Catholics did. And if there is anything true about Baptists and their Anabaptist ancestors, it is that if the Catholics do it, they don't.

Only it wasn't the end of discussion for me because what I knew as an interim minister is that short-timers can get away with most anything. What's a church going to do, fire me for suggesting we have the Lord's Supper every Sunday? They might roll their eyes, mumble behind my back. A minister would come along and rescue them. Besides, my suggestion was more modest. I proposed that after the first of the year we celebrate the meal every Sunday for one month, latter part of January into February. The basic idea of the worship series was that I would preach on different aspects of the meal each week and we would observe it in different ways. As you may know, to this day various traditions eat the meal in a variety of ways: staying seated and passing the trays or coming forward to eat it by intinction. (*Intinction* is Latin for dipping, as in dipping a piece of bread in the cup. Theologians love Latin. And Hebrew and Greek. And German.)

The folks in that church loved the idea for such a series. I suggested we begin with a Saturday night soup and salad meal at a home, watching the classic movie *Babette's Feast*, then partake of the bread and wine. And that's what we did, except with grape juice. What a lovely, quiet, and elegant time together, that Saturday evening in the home of this physician and his wife. The movie and meal moved many of us deeply. The same was true for the first Sunday of the series the next day, although I don't remember a thing about that service.

Then came the Sunday after that, February 7, 1999. Some dates you never forget. I preached from Revelation 3:20, that verse about Jesus knocking on the door of the church, wanting to come in and sup with us, a eucharistic reference if ever there was one. I hadn't always read it that way. Many of the Baptists I knew preferred to interpret the passage as Jesus wanting to be invited into our hearts, so that we might be saved. As far as I recall, no one ever wondered why it was a church's door he was knocking on, or that maybe instead of our hearts, the food reference there was literal.

My sermon was called "Table for Two," and while I emphasized the personal nature of communing with God, I didn't do justice to the corporate nature of worship at all. (The New Testament is almost always more interested in the plural form of you; the singular not so much. "Y'all" is the Texas form of Greek.) I would probably give my sermon that day a B, maybe B+ if grading on the curve. But what the Spirit of God did with that sermon, and with that meal, deserved an A+. It was almost beyond words.

But only "almost," because I have tried for years to describe what unfolded, except the problem with epiphanies is that words rarely do them justice. "You had to be there" describes most visions. But here goes: Since worshipers were to come forward and receive by intinction, and since we had four servers at two stations up front, after saying the words of institution ("On the night in which he was betrayed, Jesus took bread . . .") and inviting the people to the feast, all that remained for me to do that day was stand there looking ministerial, whatever that means.

I stood behind the table inscribed with those words about remembering Jesus, and the people started filing forward. As they did, I had a vision. Not the blurry eyes kind; more the clear eyes kind that probably had everything to do with my knowing what many of them were going through. There was Bill, the retired minister on the left side in the back pew whose wife had passed away recently. This might have even been his first Communion since her passing, and so Bill limped forward on his bad knee. There was the single mother with two kids whose husband had repeatedly cheated on her and they had divorced. She was back in church, she and her children. On and on the list went, people facing the prospects of a job loss, a malignant diagnosis, all manner of little hells. There in that little church in Arkansas, I saw broken people coming to eat broken bread and be made whole again.

"Go in peace," I said as the service concluded. Only instead of going, more people than usual flocked forward to say how moving the service had been, beyond anything they had experienced in church in a long time. Normally I might have said, "Well, thank you. The worship team puts a lot of effort into our services. I'm glad you found it meaningful." After all, my mom taught me to be gracious when someone pays you a compliment. But this was not my doing—and of course it never is—so instead I just mumbled, "I know. That was amazing, wasn't it?" So many of us had been stirred by something beyond us.

As I drove away, I thought, *This is what we are supposed to do every week.* Now when I use the word *this,* I mean the eating of the Jesus meal, not necessarily the emotional fireworks. I wasn't so naïve as to imagine that every Sunday would produce goose bumps as I dipped bread in the cup, even if I longed for such an experience. I knew then, and realize more so all these years later, meals feed us even when we aren't all that stirred by them. That's true for lasagna and salad, as well as bread and wine. Do you remember what you had for lunch two weeks ago last Tuesday? Do you remember anything special about the last time you had Communion, or the one before that? But meals feed us even when we go through the motions, because in many ways the motions go through us.

What I did know back then, and have pondered ever since, is that those earliest followers of Jesus ate this meal not only every Lord's day, but perhaps most every evening as they gathered in homes, or what we like to romanticize with the term an "upper room." I also realized I wanted to know more about those earliest followers and their meal practices.

Gathered Together

Everything you need to know about what some people call "the early church" and their upper room meal practices is tucked away in the twentieth chapter of Acts. Okay, maybe not everything; that's ministerial exaggeration. But the story we find there overflows with insights into early Christian meals, and since you could go to church your whole life and never hear this story, before you read it, a warning: it features some unusual elements. What I'm trying to say is some people think it's weird.

On the first day of the week, when we had met to break bread, Paul was holding a discussion with them; since he intended to leave the next day, he continued speaking until midnight. There were many lamps in the room upstairs where we were meeting. A young man named Eutychus, who was sitting in the window, began to sink off into a deep sleep while Paul talked still longer. Overcome by sleep, he fell to the ground three floors below and was picked up dead. But Paul went down, and bending over him took him in his arms, and said, "Do not be alarmed, for his life is in him." Then Paul went upstairs, and after he had broken bread and eaten, he continued to converse with them until dawn; then he left. Meanwhile they had taken the boy away alive and were not a little comforted (Acts 20:7–12).

It's different, right? But what a great story once you look at it closely. A number of scholars have done just that, taking a closer look at this story and the many meal narratives in the New Testament in recent years, although primarily in volumes not all that accessible to most readers. I think of Dennis Smith's *From Symposium to Eucharist*, a scholarly volume if ever there was one, a book that impacted me greatly. I want to break down this story in Acts 20, filling in some of the gaps with the help of Dennis and other scholars.[1] In attempting to translate their technical scholarship, I have tried to be faithful to them even as I hope to spark you the reader's own interest. So here are some highlights from the story in Acts 20:

"On the first day of the week . . . ." We don't usually read the books of the Bible from "cover to cover," or the book of Acts in one sitting. Of course the books of the Bible were intended to be read that way, and if we did, we might recognize this phrase, "on the first day of the week." The writer we call Luke contributed a two-volume work, the Gospel and its sequel, Acts. If we were to read all the way through both books in one sitting, we would have a better chance of seeing the connections, of how what we saw Jesus doing in the first volume we will see his followers continuing in the second. The last chapter of Luke's gospel begins with these words, "On the first day of the week . . . ," words that are now echoed. In the Gospel that final chapter is about the resurrection of Jesus, and so naturally as we begin this story, we should be expecting the same thing, someone raised from the dead. We will not be disappointed.

". . . when we met to break bread . . . ." As I noted earlier, the breaking of bread is the term Luke uses for the Eucharist, or Communion, or whatever your tradition calls it. But notice how this meal was the main reason for

gathering. When Christians "met," breaking bread was what they did. This was "worship" for them; this was "church," eating together.

"... *Paul was holding a discussion with them* ...." Those first-century dinner parties Christians inherited from Greco-Roman culture consisted of two parts, a supper (the Greek word is *deipnon*) followed by a symposium (or in Greek, *symposion*). This latter term is tricky to translate. Literally it means "drinking with," and was sometimes called the "drinking party" or "second tables." (I'm guessing that when dentists or schoolteachers or whatever group attends a "symposium" these days, the drinking parties happen after hours, not during the presentations.) In the first century a symposium was a discussion, albeit over wine after dinner. In the wider culture, these symposiums could also include musical entertainment or philosophical discussions, even political in nature. As Christians inherited and adapted this pattern, these discussions would eventually be what we call sermons today. I don't know of any congregations that print "discussion" in their bulletins as an alternative to "sermon" these days, although that's the idea here in Acts 20. But notice the preposition "with." Paul was holding a discussion *with* them. I'll have more to say about the symposium part of the evening in chapter four, "The Conversation."

"... *since he intended to leave the next day, he continued speaking until midnight* ...." Apparently, brevity was not Paul's spiritual gift. While this one seems to have drug on a bit longer than usual, first-century meal gatherings usually lasted anywhere from two-and-a-half to nearly four hours. The idea was to take life at a leisurely pace, to enjoy each other's company and not be in a hurry. Even the practice of reclining to eat was a sign of progress, not debauchery.

"... *in the room upstairs where we were meeting* ...." The phrase *upper room* carries a lot of freight for most of us, taking us back to the Gospels where Jesus eats that last supper with his friends, which might be something Luke wants in the back of our minds. In addition to echoes of resurrection, the church in Acts now eats as Jesus did with his disciples.

Of course there was nothing special about upper rooms, the opposite in fact, since these were one-room tenements in buildings four to five stories high, and where the mostly poor lived, roughly 97 percent of the population. The rooms themselves were about eighteen by twenty feet or so.

For those with the means, such rooms would have included a *triclinium*, a couch attached to the wall on three sides of the room, the fourth wall serving as entryway. These three-sided couches were nothing like the sectionals we have nowadays, lovely fabrics and textures delivered from some furniture store. Sometimes made of stone, other times of wood, they were attached to the room's walls, and when possible, covered with pads. Diners reclined lying on their left side, propped up on their left elbow, so they could eat with their right hand, typically using their hands, and not utensils. Bread was one of the ways people sopped up their food.

Because one of the couches would be against the back wall and therefore centrally located, it was considered the place of highest honor, with the middle seat on the middle couch the highest honor of all. At this meal in Acts 20, Paul was likely the guest of honor as Jesus likely would have been in the Gospel story.

"... *Eutychus, who was sitting in the window, began to sink off into a deep sleep* ...." Poor Eutychus. Everyone has trouble from time to time staying awake in church, but to fall asleep when Paul is the preacher and have Luke record it for the whole world to read. Poor Eutychus, and his name means lucky. Not very lucky, huh? This is one of the first clues that Luke means to tell us a funny story, slapstick even. One scholar calls the stories in Acts "profit with delight," meaning that while they are edifying stories, they are also meant to entertain.[2] Sometimes the entertainment is adventurous, like when the Spirit helps an apostle escape prison or the later adventures of Paul sailing the Mediterranean during a storm. This one is not so much adventurous as comedic, and likely the kind of story people retold at their own festive gatherings over a meal for years afterwards. "Hey, remember that story about the boy named Lucky, you know the one who fell ... ?"

And poor Eutychus doesn't just conk out, not right away. We get to watch as he *begins* "to sink off," heading slowly nodding down, then jerking upward. Try as he might, he can't stay awake, and all these years later everyone who reads the Bible relives him falling asleep.

This "sleep," by the way, is both literal and a kind of literary/theological reference to death, a fairly common metaphor for death in the New Testament. Now comedy gives way to tragedy in the story. The boy is dead, except Paul assures them there's no reason to be alarmed, because "his life is in him," another hint of resurrection to come.

"... *Then Paul went upstairs, and after he had broken bread and eaten* ...." Here we get a glimpse into two separate meals that had really become one. Banqueting suppers always began with the "breaking of bread," and it served as something of an appetizer before the fuller meal. Bread was broken first in the ancient world for one reason, to welcome others. The very phrase "breaking of bread" had no other meaning but sharing. Why else would you literally break off a piece of bread except to share it? This sharing signaled what the evening was about, a sharing of life together.

In terms of the room's set up, a central table would hold the evening's meal, the three staples being: bread, wine, and some kind of side dish, probably some fruit or vegetables, maybe some nuts. The wealthier might have fish or meat, even if meat sometimes caused trouble for certain Christians who associated it with idol worship. Smaller tables were positioned in front of the three couches, where diners placed their food and from which they ate. This two-hour meal was their *deipnon*, the Greek word for their supper, the main meal of the day.

When celebrating Communion, ministers typically announce, "And likewise, after the supper, he took a cup . . . ." At least that's how Paul and Luke describe it. But it's worth noting the particular wording, "after the supper." Not, "And likewise, after the bread," but "after the supper." The breaking of bread and the drinking of the cup that we now think of as Eucharist were separated by the evening meal, at least in many places. Greco-Roman society understood the bread as a sharing, not really a religious symbol so much as a cultural one. As we will see over and over, Christians adapted cultural practices, giving them religious meaning over time. The society did, however, understand this particular cup of wine in religious terms. This one glass of wine signaled the transition from the supper to symposium, a hinge moment in the evening's banquet. This cup was a drink offering called the *libation*. For those citizens who worshiped the emperor's image and perhaps other gods, this drink offering was poured out on the dirt floor or into a large bowl as an act of sacrifice, perhaps to honor Dionysius, the god of wine. For the followers of Jesus this practice of pouring out shows up in Luke's account as well, when Jesus says, "This cup that is poured out for you . . ." (Luke 22:20). Sometimes this cup was literally poured out, while at other times and in other places it seems that all those present drank the libation, and from a common cup. Remember, practices varied widely at different times and places. Among those first followers of Jesus this would become a time for remembering their Lord with a cup of wine.

"*. . . Meanwhile they had taken the boy away alive and were not a little comforted.*" As hinted at from the start, the story ends with resurrection comfort, and "not a little" either. This is satire at its best. This story as a whole is Luke's order of worship, so to speak, a narrative portrayal of what happens when we gather together. There will be the meal we now call Eucharist and the conversation we call sermon (although not usually in that order in most churches today), but also resurrection, even if more symbolic than literal.

It's common these days to name the two pillars of Christian worship: Word and Table (alas, with nothing said about music). Luke's pillars are three: meal, conversation, and resurrection. When the church gathers, there is the preaching of the word, the breaking of bread, and the raising of the dead. Eating and talking together in the presence of God enlivens us.

There is one other word we should note in this story, a wee, little word if you'll pardon the pun, namely "we." Near the beginning Luke writes, "On the first day of the week when *we* met to break bread." It's an odd practice. Writers of biblical stories didn't usually include themselves like this, using first-person plural pronouns. Luke doesn't include himself in any of his Gospel stories or in the story at Pentecost in Acts 2, not anywhere along the way. But starting a few chapters back in Acts, every once in a while Luke slips into "we" language for some of the stories. Scholars call these "we passages." There are interesting theories about these passages, including one suggestion that the author intends to include us, the readers. If so, this is Luke's way of inviting us to the table as we read.

A Real Meal

I wish I had a nickel for every time I've heard Methodists or Baptists brag about their eating habits. Presbyterians, Lutherans, Assembly of God, and Episcopalians too. All Christian traditions brag about eating. My own denomination since I had that epiphany, Disciples of Christ, same thing. Every tradition boasts, "Yeah, we eat a lot around here." They are referring of course to potluck suppers, not Communion. I've never heard anyone brag about how much bread and wine they consume during Communion. "Yeah, we encourage folks to take a big piece of Jesus." Never heard that one before. One woman I met shared how the small group at their church was always going out to eat somewhere, so they had T-shirts printed, "Small group. Big eaters." I never have the heart to tell any of these folks that all Christian denominations eat a lot.

Only if you look more closely at how we eat in our churches, it's complicated. True, some of us eat the Eucharist every week, but it's only a bite and sip at most. The potluck suppers, on the other hand, are feasts for sure—tables spread with fried chicken, green bean casseroles (I'm pretty sure those are mentioned in the Greek text of the New Testament some-where), tossed salads, cakes, and pies—but those potluck suppers are occasional at best, once every couple of months. In some ways we are a "big group, small eaters" on Sunday mornings. As one New Testament scholar cleverly observed, "It is not just that some Christians get too *much* normal food; it is that all Christians get too *little* eucharistic food. The Christian Eucharist is today a morsel and a sip. It is not a real meal."[3] And that is a real problem.

I remember one Sunday in the early 2000s arriving at a Disciples of Christ church in Kansas City, where I had been invited to preach. I arrived plenty early so as to be oriented to their eucharistic practices. (Every congregation I know seems to put their own little twist in somewhere along the way, and when you are the guest presider, it helps to know what you are doing. Failure to do so can result in outright humiliation.) The minister was away this Sunday, so the gentleman who greeted me upon arrival led me to the table. It was beautifully arranged, that much I remember. And before he lifted the silver lid from one of the serving trays, he acted as if he were the maître' d at Aixois Bistro, a fancy French restaurant in town, almost as if any moment I would behold the most gorgeous and succulent food anyone has ever seen. So after clearing his throat and setting the stage, you can imagine the disappointment when the tray was filled with those little pellets some churches use, smaller than oyster crackers really. My friend Richard calls them "Jesus pills," certainly not a mouth-watering meal.

I agree with the scholar Gordon Lathrop, who declares that even if it can't be a full meal these days, those wafers used in his own Lutheran tradition have got to go.[4] That's not a meal, Styrofoam wafers dipped in wine. Ben Witherington came to a similar conclusion in his own Methodist tradition.[5] A small bite of bread and two ounces of Welch's grape juice does not constitute a meal.

Why do we continue with this practice of merely hinting at a meal, rather than eating a real one together? A few years ago now my wife and I got involved in a small group and we decided one spring to study early Christian meals and what that might say about Communion practices now. We would study the biblical, historical, and theological aspects of this meal Christians eat. When, in the midst of that study, I noted how those earliest Christians didn't make hard and fast distinctions between their evening meals and this one in Jesus' memory, they latched onto that idea. When the study was over, we agreed to have one more session, a real-live dinner party in our home. The cuisine would be Italian, and the menu doled out to each couple, one bringing wine, another salad, another fruit, another garlic bread, and us providing the lasagna. We would eat good food, drink good wine, and share life together around a table. Then before dessert, we would pass around bread and tell stories about Jesus. My only regret is that we didn't light candles. In that upper room story about Paul and Eutychus, Luke notes, "there were many lamps in the room" (Acts 20:8). Of course oil lamps were the only means available back then, but different kinds of light matter, especially candles.

Still, the evening in our home was lovely. I offered a blessing, and we spent the next five minutes passing the food. The table talk was sometimes sports (Jordan Spieth had won the Masters earlier that day), and sometimes casual banter ("We sure are having a wet spring all of a sudden"), and sometimes political (Obamacare), and sometimes family ("How long has your daughter been dating him?"), and sometimes spiritual ("I struggle to be patient with people like that. I've been praying for patience, and now my in-laws are moving in with us. That's an answer to my prayer, I guess"). Of course, in some ways it's all spiritual, right?

When the time seemed right, I asked someone to pass me the bread we'd chosen for remembering Jesus. I didn't make a big deal of the transition, trying hard not to even make a transition at all. I simply held it up and spoke a different version of the words of institution, words not grounded in the upper room of Last Supper fame. I said, "Jesus was always breaking bread with his friends. In the wilderness with hungry crowds. On the road to Emmaus after his resurrection. When he was gathered with his friends, he would take bread and say, 'This is my body. Do this in remembrance of me.' And the same with the cup." I told them to break off a piece as we passed it around the table, much like we had passed garlic bread earlier. I also said that as we ate the bread and as we drank some wine, we should share a story about Jesus. "What's your favorite story in the Gospels?"

The bread went clockwise and the stories went every which way. My wife named the time when Jesus donned a towel and cleaned dirty feet. Patty nominated Jesus with the children, blessing them. She works with kids at the church. No surprise there. I shared two favorites, the water into wine at Cana and Jesus breaking bread in Emmaus. Those seemed fitting at a dinner party in Jesus' name.

In most worship services it's always clear when Communion is over and we are onto the next thing. But there were no such demarcations this time. We continued talking, some of us reflecting on the Gospel stories and others about a headlight burned out on their car. It was the most natural thing in the world, sharing not just bread and wine, but our lives, however mundane. Then we had dessert. I don't think it was just the wine, but even after everyone had left, I felt a warmth I have rarely felt in church. Or maybe more precisely, this was a form of church. It's no wonder Luke says the church grew as they ate their meals together (Acts 2:42–47). This was the sort of thing people would want to be part of.

The crucial point about sharing life together is not how few calories we are consuming in church but the intimacy factor, how little time we are spending together at a meal. As Norman Wirzba reminds us, the purpose of people gathering to eat isn't "to shovel nutrients into their bodies. Eating together should be an occasion in which people learn to become more attentive and present to the world and each other."[6] Food writer Adam Gopnik claims that the proliferation of cookbooks and cooking shows on TV, while indicating public interest in food, also signals the lack of quality family time over that food in their own homes. Grandparents and parents used to hand down recipes and tricks in the kitchen, then sit down to eat with each other. Gopnik compares the situation to what a book called *How to Play Catch* would reveal about our society.[7]

What does our lack of eating together as church say about the body of Christ today? Although he was not writing about eating in church, Gopnik's ideas about eating together certainly apply to us. He claims that what happens at table is more important than whether the food is organic, local, or healthy (even if those things matter). More important is the "drama" of the social table, "the people who gather at it, the conversation that flows across it, and the pain and romance that happen around it."[8] And again I say, amen.

* * *

All of this leads me to a theory I have been working on for a while, a guideline for how we might eat as church. It's something of an analogy, and of course all analogies break down, but here it is: Let us eat together in our churches the way we would eat in our homes when entertaining friends and guests. Church as a dinner party. Think about that for a moment.

Granted, when we gather as church today, it's the furthest thing from a dinner party. But it was a dinner party once upon a time, and it can be again. So what if we ate a real meal together and moved seamlessly into the

Eucharist? But let's face it, our inherited architecture is a problem. I don't necessarily mean the specific church building where your congregation gathers, although that could be true. I'm thinking more of how Christianity inherited civil basilicas under Emperor Constantine when he converted to the faith in the fourth century, and all these years later our sanctuaries feature rows of pews that often hinder face-to-face interaction, whereas we have fellowship spaces that are open, encouraging people to socialize around tables.

If you looked over our various church facilities from the perspective of an architect hovering over blueprints, it would be quite clear: here is the sanctuary on one side and the fellowship hall on the other, and never the two shall meet. That sort of separation was not initially true for the earliest followers of Jesus. But by the middle of the third century we know of one major architectural change in one city, a change symbolic of what would eventually be true in most every church today. Archaeologists discovered the remains of a house church in the city of Dura Europos, part of modern-day Syria, which apparently had a wall separating the dining room from what we would call the living room next to it. But the wall was removed at one point to create a larger meeting space, which sounds great, except the dining space was lost entirely.[9] What a tragic loss. Of course, these weren't the only architectural changes in our history. Pews would later become the norm in the Christian church, around the year 1000, even as late as the eighteenth century in parts of Europe.[10] Followers of Jesus who had once gathered around tables in small numbers became part of a large group of worshipers sitting in pews. This breaks my heart; maybe the heart of God as well. We lost a lot when we lost our dining room; and even though churches have fellowship halls today, they are quite separate from our sanctuaries.

Still, there are options for established churches to consider. One Sunday at Parkville Presbyterian Church in the suburbs of Kansas City, a congregation where I've preached several times over the years, we celebrated a joyful Eucharist in the sanctuary but that wasn't the end of the service. Rather than a benediction and the usual formalities that signal the end, we sang a song as we exited the sanctuary and recessed (or maybe we processed?) to the fellowship hall where the feasting continued.

There's no doubt in my mind that established churches can do some amazing things with their spaces as well. I once preached at St. Leonard's Parish Church in Saint Andrews, Scotland. The Sunday I preached was a Communion Sunday, and when I entered the sanctuary, it nearly took my breath away. There was wood everywhere, of course, gorgeous dark wood centuries old, along with rough stone and beautiful windows. But what made me gasp were the tablecloths. That's what I called them. I don't know if you've ever seen pews like theirs. They were shaped like every other pew I've ever seen, except instead of the one in front of you being rounded off so that worshipers might rest their hands there while singing a hymn or whatever, the back of each pew featured a small shelf about ten inches deep where worshipers might rest a hymnal or Bible. Only on this particular Sunday those shelves served as miniature tables, decked out with white linen. Even seated in traditional pews in a grand old Scottish sanctuary, it felt in some ways like we were all seated at tables.

Still, let's face it, no one has folks over for dinner in their homes, only to seat them in rows, one behind the other. Most congregations eat real meals together in their fellowship halls, so why not meet there as church gathered? I know a few congregations who have tried it with good success. Meeting at night with candles on each table might be a nice touch as well.

Or what if in some cases we were so bold as to rearrange the furniture in our sanctuaries? If you have high blood pressure, now might be the time to take your medicine. Obviously, if the congregation you're a part of meets in a grand cathedral listed on a historic register, you should disregard this suggestion. I can't imagine doing this at St. Leonard's in Scotland. But I know lots of churches where this suggestion could work. Pews are bolted to the floor, true; but The Home Depot sells wrenches.

When I visited St. Mark's Episcopal Church in Washington, DC, it was obvious they had done this very thing. According to their website, they took out the pews nearly forty years ago, and now use chairs so that worship takes place "in the round" so to speak, surrounding the altar table which is the central feature of their sacred space.

Of course new church starts and dinner churches have some clear advantages when it comes to arranging the furniture in order that they might eat together, and smaller gatherings may well be the future of Christianity. But even larger congregations often encourage small groups to meet throughout the week, most of whom wouldn't dream of getting together without snacks.

What if we encouraged these groups to eat more than Ritz crackers and cheese spread, to eat a full meal together as part of an extended evening, and move seamlessly into a time of Eucharist as well? At Country Club Christian Church, where I currently serve part-time as scholar-in-residence, small groups are being formed for just such a purpose. I recently met with the thirty or so of them who are considering hosting a dinner party with Communion as a central part of that. Of course that would entail empowering the laity, unless, as is the case in some traditions, we insist on an ordained minister presiding.

Whenever I have discussed with laypersons the idea of their presiding, in church or in homes, they admit loving the thought. Hosting a dinner party in the name of Jesus seems a lovely idea, truly. But they also admit feelings of intimidation and inadequacy. They've never presided over what in their congregation is a somewhat formal affair, depending on the traditions of their local church. What are they supposed to say? Is there a script? I usually remind them that in some ways if they've ever hosted a dinner party, they are already equipped. Some congregations are hosting dinner churches in different homes each night so that the ministers can be present at each, and while that model can work, depending on one's theology, having laypersons preside could be a powerful thing. In Shauna Niequist's lovely book *Bread and Wine*, she writes, "I want all of the holiness of the Eucharist to spill out beyond church walls, out of the hands of priests and into the regular streets and sidewalks, into the hands of regular, grubby people like you and me, onto our table, in our kitchens and dining rooms and backyards."[11] Yes, yes, yes.

Regardless of where we meet, what if we ate more bread to symbolize the abundance of God, drank more wine? If the rusty bolts holding down the pews resist the power of WD-40, or more likely, some key leaders resist changes of such a radical nature, there are still things we might try in our sanctuaries, starting with the amount of food. Bite-size pieces of bread, wafers or otherwise, won't cut it. Eating as church requires feasting. Have you read Isaiah's description of what banqueting with God looks like? "On this mountain the Lord of hosts will make for all peoples a feast of rich food, a feast of well-aged wines, of rich food filled with marrow, of well-aged wines strained clear" (Isa 25:6). Or think about that wedding in Cana where Jesus turned all that water into wine, more than one hundred gallons of the best vintage as John tells it (John 2:1–11). Larger portions signal the abundance of the good life as part of God's will for the human family.

Passing trays with miniature servings is also problematic. That practice came into vogue when grape juice replaced wine, the latter possessing an antiseptic effect. The little cups were viewed as more hygienic, even if more individualistic as well.[12] But passing the trays does have one thing going for it, something often overlooked, that we are priests to one another. The idea of passing trays is meant to suggest that the retired woman next to you can look you in the eye and utter, "The bread of life and the cup of salvation" just as meaningfully as any priest; and you in turn become priest after that for the college coed next to you. Admittedly, most worshipers don't think that way, not without some prompting from the worship leaders.

But the amount of food on those trays simply won't do. The same goes for those who dip a morsel of bread in the cup. Even the small bag of honey-roasted peanuts and a cup of Diet Coke on Southwest Airlines constitutes more food than those little crackers and thimbles of juice some churches serve. Heaven help the church if the airlines are offering more food than we are on a Sunday! Whenever possible, I think having people come forward makes more sense, because that way servers can offer larger chunks of bread, dunked in the cup ("dunked" seems more like a real meal to me than "dipped"), so that even in our sanctuaries it can feel like we are really eating. Yes, there might be crumbs on the floor, and there probably will be. That happens in our homes as well. We can always clean up afterwards.

We might also think about displays of bread on the table, loaves piled high to represent God's abundant provisions. I preached at a church some years back and in addition to stacks of bread, the worship/arts team had bread machines strategically stationed so that the smell of bread filled the room. Are there any smells better than that? And what if we got over our anal retentive obsession with planning? I preached for a Disciples of Christ congregation in the Kansas City area one Sunday that provided me a handout for how we would eat together. The handout was called "Procedures for Serving Communion." It still boggles my mind, and not because of the typos and grammatical errors. Here it is:

> After the sermon, when the elders approach the communion table, that's the deacons cue to walk forward. Stay on the lower level until the elders remove the covers from the elements. Then step up so you are all on the same level. After the elders bless the bread and the cup they will serve deacons #3 and #4, then #1 and #2. Deacons #1 and #2 keep the trays, pause a second while the elders get more trays (for themselves). Deacons #1 and #2 will step down and serve each side of the sanctuary. Deacon #4 will get their own tray and serves anyone who is unable to come forward. The #3 deacon stays behind the communion table and watches over everyone serving and replaces trays as necessary. When deacon #4

is finished serving they will return their communion trays to the table and assist deacon #3 as needed.

When deacons #1 and #2 are finished serving they return to their spots on the alter. (These deacons may finish before the elders.) Wait for your elder to return their communion trays and then serve them communion. The elders will take the deacon trays and one of the two elders will serve the minister. While the minister is being served, deacons #1 and #2 collect the offering. After the communion elements are returned to the table, one of the two deacons holding the offering plates will give the offertory prayer. After the prayer, each deacon will give their offering plate to the elder. The serving elder and deacons #2 and #4 exit to their right and the presiding elder and deacons #1 and #3 exit to their left.

Any questions? Perhaps now you see why I try to arrive early as a guest preacher, to make sure I know what's going on. You also see why lay folks in lots of congregations find serving Communion both a gratifying and terrifying act. They are afraid they'll mess up. I have also witnessed diagrams to accompany such instructions, many of those drawings resembling a playbook from the Dallas Cowboys. "You'll be the pulling guard and the running back will follow you around the left tackle." Seriously?

Can you imagine a couple in their home sweating so many details when inviting everyone to the table? "Okay, honey, let's go over this again. I'll take the pork chops, pause at the door for five seconds, then you bring the green beans in from the right side, and on my count, we will place the food on the table simultaneously." Should we synchronize our watches, too?

When I have been invited to preside over a joyful Eucharist in the sanctuary of various churches, the first thing I tell those who will be serving is not to worry. "Unless you drop the food on the floor," I tell them, "nothing can go wrong." I assure them we're not a marching band, trumpets turning to the right while the trombones veer left, everyone in lock step. What I do discuss with the servers is what they might say when serving folks (if the meal isn't primarily about Jesus' death, our language needs revising for sure), whether we are serving each other before the congregation or afterwards (a no-brainer as far as I'm concerned given my dinner party analogy), and other logistical matters. I try to reassure them, "We're feeding people. People know how to eat. You know how to hold a cup of wine or a plate of bread. Everything will be fine. And don't forget to smile."

Do things go wrong from time to time? Of course they do, just like in our homes. One server's chunk of bread is disappearing faster than the line of people. That happens when we give them more than a sliver. Someone will need to get the servers some more bread. We can figure this out. It's not rocket science. Some people think the Presbyterians coined the term about worshiping "decently and in order," when in reality they got it from Paul (1 Cor 14:40). What the apostle had in mind though was avoiding chaos in worship gatherings, not that servers needed to march in unison like soldiers on parade, somber soldiers at that.

Another thing I have pondered is, what if we treated every part of our time together as both sacred and ordinary, even the bread and wine? You don't have to be a fan of Monty Python movies to recognize the phrase, "the quest for the holy grail," a legend about the original grail or chalice that Jesus supposedly used at the Last Supper. What I'm wondering about is the ordinary grail that people used for drinking wine together, you know, a cup.

Honestly, one of the things I loved about attending seminary was learning a new language, the specialized vocabulary of the ordained, including terms such as chalice and paten. But what's wrong with a "glass" of wine and a "plate" with bread on it? Initiation into the inside language of ordained ministry can result in a separation of the spiritual life from real life. In the earliest years of Christianity, separating the two was declared a heresy that went by the name Gnosticism. The idea was that material things are somehow less spiritual. That heresy has survived down through the ages for sure.

Annie Dillard, in her beautiful meditation *Holy the Firm*, tells about suggesting to the leaders at the church where she worshiped they consider using wine instead of grape juice, which they agreed to, and then left it to her to purchase. The larger issue wasn't alcohol per se, but the holiness of the wine. It threw her for a loop at first, practically leading to apoplexy. She obsessed, "How can I buy the communion wine? Who am I to buy the communion wine? Someone has to buy the communion wine." She wondered if she should be wearing a robe, or maybe a mask in the store. "Are there holy grapes, is there holy ground, is anything here holy?" She concluded, "There are no holy grapes, there is no holy ground, nor is there anyone but us."[13] She settled for a California red, and slipped it into her backpack. In other words, as the title of her book suggests, all that is firm, all that we can see and touch and smell, is holy. The ordinary is holy. Everything is holy.

It comes as a great surprise to modern Christians to learn that our ancestors in the faith knew no such categories of *sacred* and *secular*. (To be clear, they did, however, know the category of the *profane*, a word that literally means "before the Temple," having nothing to do with religion.) Other than the profane or unclean, everything was sacred because God is everywhere and created the world "good" (Genesis 1) and Jesus became flesh; and at the same time everything was ordinary or secular because it's the real stuff of everyday life that God has named good.[14] Bottom line, we have constructed false dichotomies, sacred and secular. You can call the bread served in Communion the "host" (even if that's really God's role), but it's still bread—flour, water, salt, maybe some yeast. You know, bread. Panera sells it.

When those first followers of Jesus griped about paying taxes to Rome and in the same conversation listened to someone read the Gospel of Mark, for instance, both of those things were real. One wasn't any more religious than the other, because if you read the Gospel of Mark, you'll notice Jesus paid attention to Rome's taxation policies as well. Life is spiritual, and it's ordinary too. Must we always be transported back to an upper room in Jerusalem when Kansas City or Toledo or Boise is where we live, and Jesus keeps showing up everywhere two or three gather in his name?

For those who worry that church as dinner party entails surrendering mystery and transcendence, the very essence of traditional worship, I get that. Let me offer two images that might help counter such thinking. The first is an analogy with Wi-Fi signals. If the whole world is indeed holy, imagine the planet with Wi-Fi everywhere, every nook and cranny near and far, with a signal of the holy. But here's the catch. Just because the whole world is wired doesn't mean some spots aren't hotter than others, with a stronger signal. Dinner churches might look identical to bistros, when maybe the signal is actually stronger in these fellowships.

The other image comes from Diana Butler Bass in her book *Grounded*. For instance, she says if we think about God in relation to nature, we don't have to worship the God *apart from* nature, distant and enthroned high above. But neither must we opt for worshiping the God *of* nature, hugging trees as some kind of substitute that runs the risk of God surrendering divinity altogether. Even mystics acknowledge God is not completely accessible. Bass believes a middle way is needed, a third way, "at the horizon," that place "where heaven and ground touch, but it moves when you approach it." God with us, but at the edge.[15] God at the horizon is one of the ways people have started to rethink God's presence in terms of transcendence (distance) and immanence (nearness).

I love the story Kathleen Norris shares about how she grasped the ordinary nature of the Jesus meal in a Roman Catholic congregation, of all places, since their worship is usually quite formal. She was a lapsed Protestant herself, attending a Catholic wedding with her soon-to-be husband David. She sat in her pew during the Mass, but that didn't keep her from having an epiphany of her own. She noticed that after the meal, the priest was cleaning up, or "doing the dishes" as she put it. She writes, "I found it remarkable—and still find it remarkable—that in that big, fancy church, after all of the dress-up and the formalities of the wedding mass, homage was being paid to the lowly truth that we human beings must wash the dishes after we eat and drink."[16]

Maybe Annie Dillard should have the final word here. Elsewhere she writes, "There was never a more holy age than ours, and never a less."[17]

Dinner Church

The saying "Italy is Eataly" is more than a pronunciation guide, though helpful since the letter "i" in Italian is always pronounced like a long "e" in English. It's also more than a clever saying stitched onto T-shirts and travel bags for tourists to stock up on souvenirs. Eating is part of who Italians are at their very core. My wife and I saved money for more than ten years so that we might finally visit there. Yes, I wanted to see the ancient churches and the historic sites. Michelangelo's ceiling in the Sistine Chapel in Rome and his statue of David in Florence are beyond description. But let's face it, food was also high on our list. How can they make even the simplest plate of spaghetti melt in your mouth? I ate spoonfuls of the Parmesan cheese by itself. And the gelato, oh my. Friends had told us that the biggest meal nowadays is lunch, although that apparently is changing. One evening we enjoyed a five-course meal in the Tuscan countryside that lasted three and a half hours. Amazing.

In the first-century Mediterranean world into which Jesus was born and eventually the church, breakfast and lunch were typically light meals, and often eaten standing up at stalls of vendors. Clearly fast food is nothing new. But make no mistake, the evening meal was an occasion, especially the banquets that could last the better part of a night.

In his book *In Praise of Slowness*, Carl Honoré points out that in the 1920s Emily Post suggested a dinner party should last no longer than two and a half hours, whereas nowadays the average meal at McDonald's takes eleven minutes.[18] Faster is not always a sign of progress, even if it's a truism that the bigger something gets, the faster its pace. Think about the larger cities you know compared to smaller towns nearby, how cars move faster and people's lives as well. What if we slowed down and enjoyed each other's company?

In their thoughtful book *Slow Church*, Christopher Smith and John Pattison stress how a conversation over a dinner table may be the most important thing we do as church gathered. They write, "Specifically, we challenge you to imagine what our common life would look like if it were centered around (a) eating together at the table and (b) the slow, eucharistic conversation that convivial feasting encourages."[19] The little conjunction "and" is a key word in that sentence. It's like Panera's "pick two." We need communion *and* conversation, eating *and* talking in church. Table *and* talk.

If our ancestors in the faith likely got together most every evening of the week, or at least two to three times, that doesn't mean we have to. But we might consider what one evening a week could do for us. And gatherings at night tend to have a different pace compared to morning services anyway. In light of the kids' dance lessons, ball practice, and all the other things clamoring for our attention, an evening together with fellow believers should not be rushed. True, those first followers of Jesus didn't have a favorite TV program to get home to, but neither did they have DVRs for recording. And maybe in the end, the finale of *The Bachelor* or *The Voice* isn't really important.

I suspect what most people are hungry for today is not just enchiladas or Crab Rangoon or whatever their favorite food happens to be. And they're not just hungry for bread and wine, whatever the serving size, but fellowship. Better yet, "time with friends" or a "shared life" since the word fellowship is often romanticized, misconstrued. Maybe that's the main reason people attend churches in the first place, because getting together with folks who have similar commitments to Christ is the real deal.

If you think about it, this makes perfect sense. Why do people go to festivals and such? In Kansas City our most prominent micro-brewery is Boulevard Brewing Company, and for the last couple of years they have sponsored a festival called Boulevardia. (I know, strange name.) It features various beer tastings, food trucks, and live music. We went the first year, but couldn't even get in the next time because of high demand and space limitations. The more I have thought about such gatherings, and every community has something like it, the more I have wondered why these things are so appealing. People can buy beer in the stores much cheaper, food too. People have CDs of their favorite music already, and for the price of admission to these festivals, they could add to their music collections. So why go to festivals? To be around people, that's why. As Barbara Ehrenreich notes in her fascinating book *Dancing in the Streets: A History of Collective Joy*, we are wired to be part of people groups celebrating life.[20]

Sociologists speak about "third places," coffee shops, for instance, where people can gather in anonymity and yet still be around others. Third places come in third behind the obvious "first places," the homes where we live and "second places," where we work. But what sort of place should the church be? In many ways a lot of churches are third places, where the connections are not all that deep. What if gatherings as church were more like first places?[21]

In so many cases nowadays, churches simply slap the Eucharist onto the end of the service, a quick bite with little or no socializing. What if the meal held a more prominent place in our gatherings? If those first-century dinner parties started with food and then had a conversation while at table, what if we made eating more central and the sermon/discussion happened after that? That's not the orthodox order, I know, but who decides what is orthodox, the so-called right way? The word *heresy* by the way doesn't mean wrong, but literally "another way." Could we do church another way?

* * *

Late one spring a couple of years ago I preached in chapel at our seminary's campus in Oklahoma City, and the emphasis was on a joyful Eucharist. I'm happy to report we pulled it off, including a dialogical time of preaching, something I'll have more to say about in chapter four, "The Conversation." One of the introverts, Joanna, who used to be on staff at the seminary, told me afterwards about Dinner Church. The term caught my ear right away. "Wait, did you say 'Dinner Church'? What's that?" Turns out, the one she had in mind is a congregation in Brooklyn, St. Lydia's. Since I was going to be in New York City a few months later, I made plans to visit there. Would you turn down an opportunity to worship with a congregation that calls itself Dinner Church? Can you imagine a church where instead of someone handing you a bulletin, it's a menu instead? Well, not quite, but Dinner Church is so cool, although I realize *cool* is not a term normally used in liturgical studies. Turns out, dinner church is also a movement within Christianity here in the States and places around the world.

My good friend Lana, whom I have known since she was three, agreed to go with me to the one in Brooklyn. She and her husband Colin live in Manhattan, and so when I decided to visit Dinner Church, it was Lana and Colin who hosted me, and Lana who went with me to the worship service.

That term, *worship service*, would be a stretch for some folks if they ever experienced Dinner Church. Emily Scott started the church in 2008, although she has recently resigned and they are searching for their next pastor. It's funded in part by the ELCA, although when you visit you don't really get many Lutheran vibes. And while there's also an Episcopal connection, you don't get those vibes either. It's just church, a community of Christ followers gathered together.

Lana and I arrived at 5 PM because Emily agreed to meet and answer my many questions: How did this get started? How long has it been going? Where did you get the idea? Is it true I may have to peel carrots? What exactly is on the menu tonight? What are you preaching on?

The regulars as well as the irregulars started showing up around six, which is when you're supposed to show up, because before you can eat, the meal has to be prepared. This is pure genius, cooking together. You really get to know people in a kitchen, preparing a meal you will share. Every recipe should begin, "Gather needed ingredients and friends." Lana donned an apron. We both sliced tortillas into triangles, spreading them on cookie sheets so as to make homemade tortilla chips. After a sprinkling of olive oil and some spices, Andie, a woman who worked for the Department of Education and who was in charge of the meal that evening, threw our chips in the oven. As others arrived, plates and napkins were put in place, glasses for water or grape juice too. (They used to offer wine, but though there were some issues for recovering alcoholics, the more significant problem was too many people drinking too much. That sounds very much like what Paul describes in the ancient church at Corinth.) Andie stirred a delicious pot of rice, tomatoes, cilantro, and who knows what else. My batch of chips was a bit too salty, although no one complained.

While some of us were cooking and setting up, others were rehearsing their various parts in the evening's service. Worshipers don't really receive a printed order of worship, although those who are leading do. You can find a sample at their website if you simply Google "Dinner Church," although I'm told the service is not always the same. What I remember most is how the bread is broken before the meal and the cup received afterwards. Well, that and how since nothing is really printed for those present, everything is sung or said by a leader, then repeated by those gathered. I really remember more than that, but it's one of those things where you have to be there to experience it. For instance, I remember the candles we all lit then placed on the tables. Candle-lit dinners often spark images of romance, and in a way that's what Dinner Church is, a romance among those gathered as well as between God and us.

I was somewhat surprised at how many of those gathered had theological degrees of one sort or another. They weren't all in vocational ministry per se, but they were theologically articulate for sure. (I've learned since then that a lot of dinner churches around the country attract pastors who are looking for such a gathering on a day off, especially one where they don't have to lead.) At St. Lydia's the conversations ranged all over the place—politics, weather, Scripture, church—sacred and secular rolled into one. I had spent the weekend going from one eatery to another with Colin and Lana, taking pictures of some of the bistros. When I snapped a photo of Dinner Church, anyone flipping through my smart phone would have easily confused this church with a restaurant. I can think of worse comparisons.

My one hesitation with Dinner Church was the way we moved from eating that rice dish into something of a more formal liturgy, albeit a beautiful and ancient one borrowed from the Didache, an early church document from around the end of the first century. Transitions where ministers clear their throats and signal a move from one thing to another often put a damper on what I think really should flow more seamlessly during the church's dinner party. It's true that as our ancestors in the faith moved from supper to symposium, some transitions took place, including tables moved back, floors swept, and a ceremonial washing of hands, but apparently they were able to maintain a sense of holy and mundane held in tension rather than separated.[22] For us, transitions often send the wrong signal, shifting from a time of intimate sharing over a meal to a more formal time of worship. But as we shall see, there are lots of dinner church models, some more formal and others less, especially in terms of eating the bread and wine. Some dinner churches feature a formal, or high, Eucharistic theology, whereas others have a less formal, or lower, one. (Honestly, categories of high and low may not be very fair assessments these days.)

When one of my former students, Joy, and her husband, Elliott, decided to adapt the model of Dinner Church with the college and career group in their church, they struggled with this very thing: how does one seamlessly move from eating to, well, more eating? And how can that happen without people feeling like they are moving from a secular to a more sacred (and therefore, serious) part of their time together? One of our biggest struggles is not just transitions but the words of institution we use, "For I received from the Lord what I also handed on to you, that the Lord Jesus on the night when he was betrayed took a loaf of bread . . ." (1 Cor 11:23). Even on paper right here, these words often signal a certain tone, that no matter what has happened in worship up until this moment, now it's time to get serious, to get holy, to recognize a so-called sacred act.

Except those are not the only words of institution in the New Testament. Paul's version is not the same as Luke's, which is different from Matthew's, and so on. That diversity alone is enough to encourage us to try different ways as well.[23] Traditionally, churches have used only one version of framing the Jesus meal, the story from the night before his death, a Maundy Thursday version. But what about all the other meal references? What if those inspired different ways of framing the meal? (At the end of the book I suggest different ways we might formulate the words of institution, different images for framing the meal.) For example, in churches where I've been introducing a joyful eucharistic feast, I have sometimes referred to the feeding stories in the wilderness, using historical present tense verbs, which feels more present than historical:

> The New Testament talks about this meal in many ways other than those of the Last Supper in that upper room. When Jesus feeds 5,000 people in the wilderness, all four of the Gospel writers use language of how he took bread, gave thanks, broke it, and gave it to them. So hear different words as we come to this table today:

> When Jesus is with his friends, he takes bread, gives thanks, breaks it, and gives it to them, to us. We are his body, and we eat in remembrance of him. And likewise he takes a cup, gives thanks, and gives it to them, to us. We drink in remembrance of him.[24]

One of those churches where I introduced a joyful Eucharist is Pine Ridge Presbyterian in Kansas City. The minister, Jim Gordon, is a good friend, and although he was away that Sunday, he loved the idea of a joyful Eucharist. So after the sermon that helped set that up, and after a different version of the words of institution, we feasted together. When the people had finished coming forward and were still visiting with each other, I asked, "Did everyone get something to eat?" They paused in their fellowshipping with one another, smiled, and spontaneously began clapping. I didn't see that coming. Even in that spacious and traditional sanctuary, it felt like a dinner party. Not every congregation is going to morph into a dinner church or even offer alternative dinner church services, but any congregation could make their eucharistic meal feel more like a dinner party.

CHAPTER 2

The Guest List

"And they shall come from east and west, and from north
and south, and shall recline at table in the reign of God."

—Luke 13:29 (author's translation)

Eating Your Way through the Gospels

Maybe you've heard the joke: What did Jesus say at the Last Supper? "Okay, fellows, everyone who wants to be in the picture, move over on this side of the table." The iconic painting's portrayal of how they ate in the first century is not the least bit historically accurate, although seated upright at a table likely reflects how people ate in Da Vinci's time. As we've already noted, in the first-century Mediterranean world most people ate their evening meals reclining on couches that lined three walls of the room. Even if Jesus had gathered his followers around rectangular tables the way we do in our fellowship halls, it wouldn't have been on only one side. But as my art professor friend Rob once told me, Da Vinci's version allows all who look at it to join Jesus and his disciples at the meal. What an interesting take on that classic piece of art, and it's also very much in line with the notion of who gets invited to the table.

In his little book *Eating Your Way through Luke's Gospel*, Robert Karris famously writes that on nearly every page, "Jesus is either going to a meal, at a meal, or coming from a meal."[1] It's only the slightest of exaggerations. Try flipping through the pages of Luke and you'll see. In Luke's gospel alone, Karris identifies fifty different references to food and forty-five different words related to eating and foods. Luke's vocabulary marks him as the foodie among the four Gospel writers, no question. If we had an illustrated version of the third Gospel, Jesus might be pictured wiping his face with his sleeve, crumbs falling from his beard.

As I noted earlier, Greco-Roman banqueting is everywhere in the New Testament because that's the way they ate their evening meals. Here are just a few examples from the third Gospel, with glimpses into the banqueting tradition we've been considering. Early in his ministry Jesus surprisingly calls a despised tax collector (or more likely, a toll collector) named Levi to follow him. It's surprising because Levi had betrayed his own Jewish friends and kin to work for the oppressive Romans. The man would sit in a roadside booth, collecting tolls not by means of some fair formula, but taking whatever he could get away with. Can you imagine pulling up to a tollbooth nowadays only to have the collector look over the make of car you're driving before deciding what to charge? "Oh, Chevy Tahoe, huh? Let's see, that will be . . . ."

What's even more surprising is that Jesus then goes to eat in the home of Levi. Luke writes, "Then Levi gave a great banquet for him in his house; and there was a large crowd of tax collectors and others sitting at the table with them" (Luke 5:29). Not only do we read of a "great banquet," but the meal takes place in a house big enough for large crowds, all of whom are reclining there (not "sitting"). When the religious leaders object on the grounds that he is eating with the wrong kind of folks, Jesus replies, "I have come to call not the righteous but sinners" (Luke 5:32). The word translated "call" is actually the same word they used for issuing invitations to banquets, which is really odd for Jesus to say since he's the guest at this particular meal, and yet it's a fascinating theological statement, a way for Luke to proclaim Jesus' willingness to eat with "those sorts of people."

A few pages later Luke describes another banquet (Luke 7:36–50), this one in the home of Simon the Pharisee. It's only in Luke's gospel that Jesus eats with Pharisees. Here's how that evening is described: "One of the Pharisees asked Jesus to eat with him, and he went into the Pharisee's house and took his place at the table" (Luke 7:36). So much of the language of banqueting is once again lost to us in translation. Jesus is not just "asked," but in the Greek is *invited*. And once there, Jesus doesn't just take his place but reclines at the table, likely on the couch of honor since he is a special guest. The scene continues when a woman of the city hears about the banquet and crashes the party, so to speak. This is an indication of how banqueting was rarely private because doors and windows didn't really exist the way we think of them now. Anyone passing by someone's house would have witnessed such banquets going on, even wandered in on occasion.

Over and over in the pages of Luke's gospel, Jesus eats. What is most striking, however, is not *how often* Luke tells about Jesus eating, but *who he eats with*. In a phrase, pretty much anyone who will have him. We don't know if he had a discriminating palate, but he definitely didn't have a discriminating list of folks with whom he was willing to eat. Thus, the pejorative label, a "friend of tax collectors and sinners" (Luke 7:34), a nickname Jesus likely wore proudly. If you were one of the Pharisees who leaned toward isolating oneself from such company (and not all Pharisees did), you could hold that against him; but it worked the other way around too, since Jesus ate with the religious leadership as well as the outcasts.[2]

In Luke's Gospel, Jesus also tells a story about an extravagant dinner party while he was at just such a party himself. It's the story of a father who had two sons, what we sometimes call the parable of the Prodigal Son (Luke 15:11–32).[3] I probably don't need to rehearse the whole thing here, but the basic plot wouldn't hurt as a refresher. Jesus tells about a father whose younger son asks for his inheritance in advance, only to leave town as soon as his request is granted. The boy squanders it all, endures a famine, during which no one offers him any assistance, and when he finds himself longing to eat pig slop, decides he would be better off back at home even if his dad only took him back as a slave. Except the father receives him back as an honored son, throwing a party and preparing a lavish feast.

As you may recall, the older son who has not left home but continued to work for his dad all along is not exactly happy to hear of his brother's return, especially the party. Returning from a day in the field, he hears "music and dancing," although I have no idea how you can *hear* dancing. He refuses to go in, so the dad comes out on the porch, where they discuss the merits of such a party.

For years I read this story as a challenge to the religious establishment—Jewish or Christian—when we stand at the door and instead of being greeters, act as bouncers. My sermons along these lines encouraged us to embrace the wayward, the rebellious, the homeless man who smells, the drug addict with all those piercings.

Then it hit me: the wayward younger son and his father are *inside* the house partying. The older brother is *outside* on the porch. David May, my good friend and New Testament scholar, says it's not just *who* is inside, but *what* they are inside, namely a house. David's doctoral dissertation explored the use of "house" in the Gospels. The theory is that since by the time the Gospels were written and the Jesus movement was long established as a house movement, stories in the Gospels about the "house" were meant to be heard as church stories.[4] Reading the story this way, a picture emerges of religious folks like me missing out. And to think Jesus told this story while eating with despised toll collectors, responding to the grumblings of the deacons and elders, I mean, the Pharisees.

I previously suggested we might conceive of the church's eating together as a dinner party. This is one of the places where the analogy breaks down. In her book *Eating Together*, sociologist Alice Julier catalogues a variety of meals we enjoy regularly in the United States. She's not interested in just any meals, but the social kind—formal dinner parties, potluck suppers, the backyard barbecue, and so forth.[5] Each one has at least two things in common, the social and the gastronomical. Other than that, they are quite different in terms of the kinds of food, who might contribute what, how organized the time together becomes.

As I read her work, I was struck with where the church's early eating practices might come in. At one point she describes a kind of middle ground between formal dinner parties and potluck suppers, what she calls "having friends over." People can bring things, although the party doesn't depend on it. There is no prescribed seating arrangement, and folks might spend more time in the kitchen than in the dining room (which might help to explain why so many house hunters on HGTV want an open concept). Friends have gathered to express their love for each other, even if no such words are ever spoken. They are part of what it means to be together, to share stories and share a meal.

Maybe that's more like what the church does, only here is the crucial difference: the circle is always drawn wide at God's table. It's also why the dinner church model shouldn't be compared to a family dinner; not just because so many family dinners bring up horribly dysfunctional homes, although that's true, but because family dinners imply only some belong to the family. God's family is bigger than we have imagined. This too points to why some dinner churches opt to meet in restaurants and more public places than in homes. Not only are homes limited in space, but someone is the owner of that place while a more neutral site implies no ownership by one person or family. House churches and dinner churches are obviously similar, but certainly not identical.

I remember years ago a colleague making the distinction between the people you have over for dinner willingly as opposed to under some compulsion. A wife says to her husband, "I know he's a prick, but he's my boss. We really should have him and his wife over some time. I'll make it up to you." That's a very different scenario from, "Call David and Pam; see if they want to join us. Dan and Janet, too. We'll be outside, so there's plenty of room. See if Drew and Lindsey want to come as well." It is intolerable to think of the church's weekly gathering as a dinner party where only some of our closest friends are welcome. As one scholar observes, our table practices constitute "society's miniature mirror."[6]

The problem with the dinner party analogy isn't the format, the food, the festive time. The problem is who gets invited. Jesus even had something to say about this when he attended another banquet exclusively attended by Pharisees and suggested that the guest list should include the most unlikely of persons: the poor, crippled, lame, and blind (Luke 14:12–14). You can imagine how well that went over. He said if hosts have to, they should go out and invite folks off the street so that the banquet is full. I'm surprised anyone ever wanted to host Jesus for dinner. The church's version of "having friends over" is that all are welcome, and not just the outcasts either, but even the pricks, because, well, some of us are pricks too. Norman Wirzba reminds us, "Though we may not always like the people we are with or the food on our plates, we cannot deny them entirely because they are the indispensable *sources* of our life together."[7]

This leads to a very subtle but important point, one that I've had fun making on retreats with church leaders over the years. A pastor and some key lay leaders in a congregation will ask me to lead them in a study, a day or two apart at some denominational retreat center to talk about revitalizing their worship. At one point I ask, "Do you have greeters at your church?" They proudly announce that they do, thinking I'll give them a gold star, check that off the list. But of course every church I know has greeters, some more trained than others. Still, churches have greeters, par for the course. Then comes the trick question, "Why? Why do you have greeters?" You should see them struggle, furrowed brows. Such an easy and yet difficult question. In part, they can't imagine why I don't know the answer. But they also struggle to find words that justify the existence of greeters. Eventually one of them will respond, "So people will know we are friendly, that they are welcome." That's when I press them further, "But *why* are you friendly? The greeter at Walmart is friendly too. What's the difference?" Silence. I then suggest that the church welcomes the stranger not because we're called to be friendly, welcoming someone to *our* church, but because it is *God's* church in the first place. We welcome the stranger because that's how we got in—God welcomed us.

Guess Who's Coming to Dinner

Whenever I lead a Bible study on eating in the early church, I typically invite folks to name passages of Scripture we might consider. The list is fairly predictable. No one ever nominates the story of the tower of Babel in Genesis 11, and for good reason; it's not about the Jesus meal, or any other meal. But it is where I'd like for us to look briefly because it has something to say about how we tend to view "others." Here's the story from Genesis 11:

> Now the whole earth had one language and the same words. And as they migrated from the east, they came upon a plain in the land of Shinar and settled there. And they said to one another, "Come, let us make bricks, and burn them thoroughly." And they had brick for stone, and bitumen for mortar. Then they said, "Come, let us build ourselves a city, and a tower with its top in the heavens, and let us make a name for ourselves; otherwise we shall be scattered abroad upon the face of the whole earth." The Lord came down to see the city and the tower, which mortals had built. And the Lord said, "Look, they are one people, and they have all one language; and this is only the beginning of what they will do; nothing that they propose to do will now be impossible for them. Come, let us go down, and confuse their language there, so that they will not understand one another's speech." So the Lord scattered them abroad from there over the face of all the earth, and they left off building the city. Therefore it was called Babel, because there the Lord confused the language of all the earth; and from there the Lord scattered them abroad over the face of all the earth.

It's fairly common to think of this passage singling out pride as the sin of humanity, as if some egotistical real estate developer wants to build a tower that reaches high into the sky, and on the surface it looks as if God is worried about the competition. But I don't think that's the main idea, even if it is a part. I think this passage is about one word, *xenophobia*. Yes, another Greek word, "fear of the stranger." Here's why I think that's the main idea.

For starters, in the story the people set out to build a tower so that they can stay there, settle down, not be "scattered abroad." That is the reason behind their building project. The English translation there sounds punitive, being scattered, whereas it might better read "dispersed." And where the text says that God "confused the language," it might better be translated as "mixed." In other words, God's plan was to have diverse peoples with different languages rubbing elbows and mingling, not gated communities among like-minded folks or walls along borders to keep out the so-called alien. By the way, international travel is still a great cure for xenophobia!

For whatever reason, fear of the stranger is in the genes we inherit and the air we breathe, nature and nurture. From the time we were kids building forts out of couch cushions or tree houses ten feet off the ground, one of the first things we did as we crawled inside was set up rules for who wouldn't be admitted. In order to feel like we really belonged, someone had to be excluded. That kid with braces, the bullies who picked on us, little sisters and little brothers, you name it. We pulled a sheet down over the cushions or the rope ladder in behind us. "No one else."

Unfortunately, the church does that with food, the eucharistic food at least. We will gladly let even perfect strangers join us in the fellowship hall for fried chicken and homemade pies, but at the table in our sanctuaries where we proclaim God's grand welcome in the context of worship, around that table we have erected barriers. "No bread and wine for *you*. This is about God's love for *us*."

There's another fascinating little story Luke tells, another meal story tucked away near the end of Acts, a tale of Paul's sea voyage on the Mediterranean. Like the story of Eutychus in chapter 20 that we looked at, this is another "we story." And also like the story of Eutychus, this one is a bit odd on the surface.

Remember, the stories in Acts are meant to be entertaining as well as edifying, and whereas the one about the boy named Lucky who falls out the window is somewhat slapstick, now we encounter real drama, a storm at sea. I'll just quote a few lines from Acts 27 to capture some of the flavor, while you try to smell the salt air:

> When it was decided that we were to sail for Italy, they transferred Paul and some other prisoners to a centurion of the Augustan Cohort, named Julius. Embarking on a ship of Adramyttium that was about to set sail to the ports along the coast of Asia, we put to sea, accompanied by Aristarchus, a Macedonian from Thessalonica

(vv. 1–2). . . . We sailed slowly for a number of days and arrived with difficulty off Cnidus, and as the wind was against us, we sailed under the lee of Crete off Salmone (v. 7). . . . When a moderate south wind began to blow, they thought they could achieve their purpose; so they weighed anchor and began to sail past Crete, close to the shore. But soon a violent wind, called the northeaster, rushed down from Crete. Since the ship was caught and could not be turned head-on into the wind, we gave way to it and were driven (vv. 13–15). . . . We were being pounded by the storm so violently that on the next day they began to throw the cargo overboard, and on the third day with their own hands they threw the ship's tackle overboard. When neither sun nor stars appeared for many days, and no small tempest raged, all hope of our being saved was at last abandoned (vv. 18–20).

After this Paul gives a little speech about how they should have listened to him and not set sail when they did. I'm not sure that's a good idea, giving speeches to your captors that in essence say, "I told you so." He does assure them that even if the ship is destroyed, no one will be harmed because God has plans for Paul to make it to Rome. After that, the sailors begin to take soundings, trying to see if they're in danger of running aground on the rocks nearby. It looks really bad, so the sailors hatch a scheme to escape in one of the lifeboats while they pretend to be setting some anchors. Paul then makes another speech, addressed to the Roman soldiers on board, "Unless these men stay in the ship, you cannot be saved" (v. 31). Note the religious language there.

What happens next is hard to believe in some ways. Here's how Luke describes it:

Just before daybreak, Paul urged all of them to take some food, saying, "Today is the fourteenth day that you have been in suspense and remaining without food, having eaten nothing. Therefore I urge you to take some food, for it will help you survive; for none of you will lose a hair from your heads." After he had said this, he took bread; and giving thanks to God in the presence of all, he broke it and began to eat. Then all of them were encouraged and took food for themselves (Acts 27:33–36).

By now, I'm guessing it would be hard for you to miss the eucharistic reference here, Paul's taking bread, giving thanks, breaking it, and so forth. This bread will help them "survive," help *save* them is how the Greek reads. That word *saved* is not about a ticket to heaven, saved from hell. No, it's best translated as "made whole." This meal will make them whole, that's what the New Testament means by salvation. It's also hard to miss how this eucharistic reference occurs between an apostle and some sailors under the supervision of Roman soldiers. Luke's outdoor church at sea apparently has an open door policy when it comes to Communion. Everyone is welcome at God's table, as Luke tells it.

* * *

You're probably familiar with the term "closed Communion," the notion that some persons are not welcome at the Lord's table for a variety of reasons. Maybe it's being part of another denomination. Or being a member of another local church. It's an ancient practice, early as the end of the first century when the unbaptized were excused from that portion of the service, at least in some places. Never mind the fact that at the so-called Last Supper, Jesus fed Peter, who would deny him, and Judas, who would hand him over.

There are historical and theological reasons for how this developed, this notion of the meal being only for the baptized, only for the church. A person could read thousands of pages about those developments. At the same time, there are good reasons for letting anyone eat this meal, reasons that are also historical and theological in nature. As you might guess, both positions have been held and espoused from the beginning until now. Thus, the usual arm-wrestling match, and with no clear winners. Each of us has to decide for ourselves.

Cindy, a minister friend of mine in the Kansas City area, has decided for sure. She used to teach theology at Notre Dame de Sion, a Catholic girls' school. Understandably most of the girls were Catholic, but there were also some Protestants who recognized the school as excellent preparation for college. Occasionally there were even some Muslims, Jews, and Hindus in her classes. One year, she had a sophomore class getting ready to attend an all-school Mass. As faculty, she was charged with the responsibility of preparing students for each liturgy, which also included explaining how only Catholic girls would be allowed to receive Communion. This particular day she had a student who was a practicing Hindu, who put her hand up and asked directly, "Why is it that only Catholics can receive Communion? I have been a student here for almost two years and I have learned a lot about what Catholics believe. I think I understand that Communion is about receiving Jesus."

A hush fell over the room. Before Cindy could say anything, a couple of girls immediately explained to her that they had spent a great deal of time when they were younger preparing for "First Communion." You couldn't just go because you felt like it. You had to go through special preparation and learn more about what it really meant. The young woman responded, "I think I understand what it means. I guess I was just curious. I always feel like I'm an outsider when we go to Mass. I was just wondering is all."

Cindy told me that it shouldn't have surprised her when at Communion time this young Hindu woman went up to receive. The rest of her class looked on in horror. Cindy knew there would be a discussion when they got back to the classroom. Sure enough, the Catholic girls were up in arms. "Can you believe she went right up there and went to Communion? What are you going to do about it? What is going to happen?" They were appalled and even angry. The girl herself was the picture of calm. Cindy reassured everyone that there would be no thunderclap of judgment. This young woman had been curious, and she had satisfied her curiosity. They would leave it up to Jesus. Period. End of conversation. Except it wasn't of course.

By the next morning, Cindy received three phone calls from parents of students. "What are you doing, allowing girls of other faiths to receive Communion?" One noted, "She's not even a Christian!" Finally, Cindy invited each of them to come to class and observe the nature of religious instruction that their daughters were receiving. Some of them did just that, and after visiting classes, they realized their daughters were getting exactly what they wanted for them, an education in which they explored issues of religious faith, deciding for themselves what they would believe. Cindy told me that ever since she has been in touch with the girl, now thirty-something and a physician. She said, "I respect her deeply."

By the way, the opposite of *xenophobia* in Greek is *philoxenia*. In contrast to "fear of the stranger," it means "love of the stranger." But here's the really great part. Most translators of the New Testament use a different English word when translating *philoxenia*, not "love of the stranger," but "hospitality." What a great word.

Table Manners

Some folks are surprised to discover that the earliest written account of the Jesus meal is not in the Gospels, but in one of Paul's letters to the church in Corinth. The Apostle "mailed" his letter a good fifteen years ahead of

Mark's writing the first Gospel ever, even if stories about that so-called Last Supper had been circulating for a long time. This is one of those cases when chronological and canonical order gets confusing.

Unfortunately, Paul's account is also the most misunderstood, and this misunderstanding has hung over Lord's Supper services ever since, resulting not only in a somber observance but causing many of us to fixate on the wrong thing entirely when it comes to eating this meal. Of course, in a way it's understandable how it happened. When a passage warns against eating in an "unworthy manner," and oh by the way, how that could result in illness, or even death, it's easy to see how this meal often resembles a funeral more than a dinner party. Can you imagine telling people over a formal dinner that if they confuse the salad fork with the dessert fork, it could be the last thing they ever do? I can see how that might put a damper on a dinner party.

The problem with Paul's passage isn't what he teaches, but how we have misunderstood his teaching. So let's take a closer look at the familiar part of Paul's passage, and then the less familiar context. Here's the passage most of us know, words that are often cited on Sunday mornings in worship services, at least the first part of it:

> For I received from the Lord what I also handed on to you, that the Lord Jesus on the night when he was betrayed took a loaf of bread, and when he had given thanks, he broke it and said, "This is my body that is for you. Do this in remembrance of me." In the same way he took the cup also, after supper, saying, "This cup is the new covenant in my blood. Do this, as often as you drink it, in remembrance of me." For as often as you eat this bread and drink the cup, you proclaim the Lord's death until he comes. Whoever, therefore, eats the bread or drinks the cup of the Lord in an unworthy manner will be answerable for the body and blood of the Lord. Examine yourselves, and only then eat of the bread and drink of the cup. For all who eat and drink without discerning the body, eat and drink judgment against themselves. For this reason many of you are weak and ill, and some have died. But if we judged ourselves, we would not be judged. But when we are judged by the Lord, we are disciplined so that we may not be condemned along with the world (1 Cor 11:23–32).

No wonder some folks are fearful when eating this meal. But now the larger context. In the verses just before this Paul writes:

> When you come together, it is not really to eat the Lord's supper.
> For when the time comes to eat, each of you goes ahead with your
> own supper, and one goes hungry and another becomes drunk.
> What! Do you not have homes to eat and drink in? Or do you
> show contempt for the church of God and humiliate those who
> have nothing? What should I say to you? Should I commend you?
> In this matter I do not commend you! (1 Cor 11:20–22)

And after those familiar verses, we read this:

> So then, my brothers and sisters, when you come together to
> eat, wait for one another. If you are hungry, eat at home, so that
> when you come together, it will not be for your condemnation.
> About the other things I will give instructions when I come (1 Cor
> 11:33–34).

This is where I need to take us back to that Christmas break when our
kids were home and I was reading those books about ancient banqueting,
because there is one dynamic we simply must grasp to understand Paul's
context. It has everything to do with their homes, specifically the different kinds of dwellings in the first century. Consider this the first-century
Mediterranean version of HGTV's *House Hunters*, the international one.
Only instead of some couple trying to decide between three vacation villas
in Belize (with granite countertops and stainless steel appliances of course),
we will look at the three types of homes that existed back then—apartments, condos, and mansions.[8]

As I noted earlier, the overwhelming majority of people, Christian
or otherwise, were poor, and they lived in what we so romantically label
"upper rooms." These apartments were one-room dwellings in buildings
sometimes as high as four or five stories, with the poorest conditions often existing the higher up you went. People didn't cook or even defecate
in these most basic apartments; they mostly slept in them or stored stuff
there. The ground floor apartments, however, likely doubled as shops. In
the typical apartment building, some of the tenements might have included those three-sided couches for entertaining, while that would have
been out of the question for the poorest of the poor.[9] Whether the story of
Eutychus in Acts 20 took place in such an apartment is hard to know for
sure. It certainly seems likely, especially with the reference to his falling
three stories below.

Condos were for the wealthier members of society, U-shaped buildings with several units that looked out onto a central garden or courtyard.

These homes were more luxuriously appointed and would have featured a dining room for reclining at meals with a large number of guests, not just small groups. (That toll collector Levi likely lived in one of these, and maybe Simon the Pharisee as well.)

The mansions were of course even larger, with tapestries and mosaics in the floor, a kind of first-century version of rugs. (Perhaps Zacchaeus, the only *chief* toll collector mentioned in the New Testament, lived in one of these. In Luke 19:1–10 there's a story of Jesus going to eat in Zacchaeus's home, and leading to his salvation, or being made whole.) These grand mansions not only featured large dining rooms lined with three-sided couches, but other spaces where large crowds might spill out to eat on special occasions. Some evidence suggests that at the larger gatherings one's standing indicated which room you were in. Not unlike the kids' table at Thanksgiving in many a home in the United States.

We know that the church at Corinth, or maybe more accurately, the various house churches scattered throughout the city, included both rich and poor. Early in this same letter to the Christians there, Paul writes, "not many of you were wise by human standards, not many were powerful, not many were of noble birth" (1 Cor 1:26). If *not many* of them were, then at least some of the members were powerful and quite wealthy.[10] Two patterns of meals emerged, depending on who hosted the meal and where, patronal and potluck.

We know potluck in our churches. Apparently it's an ancient practice. In their potluck meals, Eucharist included, they shared what food they had, each bringing something to throw into the mix. Patronal meals were different, with wealthier members providing all the food, clearly the case in Paul's context. Here's why I say that: the poorer members who worked long hours in various occupations would naturally arrive later than the wealthy, some of whom no longer had to work at all or who negotiated business deals while banqueting. The result? The food was picked over so that the poorer members had little or nothing to eat, while the rich were not only patting full tummies, but also starting to feel a buzz from the wine.

Paul's critique begins to make much more sense in this light. When he talks about "discerning the body" (1 Cor 11:29), he's not referring to our bodies and whatever sins we might have committed but the church as the body of Christ. Have all the members of this body been fed? That is Paul's main concern, and he's not happy about it. For some of these poorer members, this might well be their only food for the day. That is what he means by an "unworthy manner."

And there's more. As my English teachers reminded me as far back as junior high, there's a big difference between an adjective and adverb, an especially important distinction here. This passage doesn't say anything about people being *worthy* (adjective), but about the way we take it being *worthily* (adverb), in a "worthy manner" as some translations rightly put it. And for Paul, such worthiness is measured by how many of the poorer members have been fed, not just the fat cats.

It seems to me a misreading of this portion of Paul's letter is mostly to blame for the funeral-like Communion services we now endure, the ones where not only the lights are lowered, but spirits too, as we are encouraged to inventory the sins we have committed since last we gathered. But what kinds of sins?

One time I was in Michigan for their annual Calvin Symposium on Worship. I've attended and been a presenter there several times, and it's always a delight. Like a lot of conferences, participants sit at round tables of eight or so at mealtime. On this particular occasion after we had introduced ourselves and moved from one topic to another, we eventually landed on Communion practices. One of those persons whose tradition I no longer recall shocked us all when he said guests at his church must interview with the pastor prior to services in order to partake. I nearly choked on my corn flakes. We asked all the questions you might imagine, including when exactly this interview would take place, and so forth. I finally asked, "And what sorts of things would be included in the interview, what sorts of questions?" I was playing dumb, because I had an educated hunch. So before he could answer I said, "Wait, let me guess," and then switched into satire mode. "Maybe things like whether that person has been moved to care for the poor or has been indifferent toward the homeless and hungry. Or maybe things like whether that person has worked for immigration reform, the plight of the stranger in our midst." He looked at me as if I were from another planet. "No, nothing like that. More like if they have lusted in their heart, been faithful to their spouse. Are they divorced and now remarried." Funny how the only "sins" this pastor cared about are ones sexual in nature. I think Paul would be very disappointed in that sort of inquisition, nothing about the poor and marginalized in our world.

Many of us would be shocked to discover there are people in our churches barely putting food on the table, assuming we haven't shamed them into staying away altogether. I wonder what we might envision in our churches where the Eucharist and food pantry were combined into one religious act. In her book *Take This Bread*, Sara Miles describes starting a food pantry in her church in the Bay Area, one where she insisted that the distribution take place at the same altar where the Eucharist was served every Sunday.[11] But what if the food pantry and Eucharist were seamlessly woven together? I've seen churches that combine the offering with Communion, worshipers coming forward to eat, and dropping money into baskets before returning to their seats. We certainly don't want to embarrass those in need, making them take food items with everyone watching. But what if after eating Communion on Sunday, we had food available as well, and it was up front with the remnants of our bread and wine? Or what if our offering for the poor was somehow connected to the Eucharist?[12]

The Welcome Table

One of the problems with how we read the books of the Bible is doing so in small bite-sized chunks rather than digesting the whole thing the way it was intended. For example, we read Mark's gospel one Sunday in church, isolating six verses here or eight verses there from a chapter smack dab in the middle of his larger story, unaware of what went on before and what will follow. Sometimes I show my students at the seminary how strange this practice is with a demonstration from a novel. I'll bring my copy of *The Grapes of Wrath* or *To Kill a Mockingbird*, something they read once upon a time, or were supposed to anyway. (This seems analogous to the reading of Scripture for some people.) I announce, "Today's reading is from *Mockingbird* 3:16" and begin reading the sixteenth line in chapter 3 or some such thing. Even for those who know the story well, it feels odd jumping into the larger story so abruptly.

Something similar happens near the middle of Mark's gospel with the story of the feeding of the multitudes, a story carefully woven into the fabric of his whole Gospel narrative. So let's start with the feeding narrative and move out from there because while it might not seem like it, it has everything to do with the meal we call Communion. The story goes like this:

> The apostles gathered around Jesus, and told him all that they had done and taught. He said to them, "Come away to a deserted place all by yourselves and rest a while." For many were coming and going, and they had no leisure even to eat. And they went away in

the boat to a deserted place by themselves. Now many saw them going and recognized them, and they hurried there on foot from all the towns and arrived ahead of them. As he went ashore, he saw a great crowd; and he had compassion for them, because they were like sheep without a shepherd; and he began to teach them many things. When it grew late, his disciples came to him and said, "This is a deserted place, and the hour is now very late; send them away so that they may go into the surrounding country and villages and buy something for themselves to eat." But he answered them, "You give them something to eat." They said to him, "Are we to go and buy two hundred denarii worth of bread, and give it to them to eat?" And he said to them, "How many loaves have you? Go and see." When they had found out, they said, "Five, and two fish." Then he ordered them to get all the people to sit down in groups on the green grass. So they sat down in groups of hundreds and of fifties. Taking the five loaves and the two fish, he looked up to heaven, and blessed and broke the loaves, and gave them to his disciples to set before the people; and he divided the two fish among them all. And all ate and were filled; and they took up twelve baskets full of broken pieces and of the fish. Those who had eaten the loaves numbered five thousand men (Mark 6:30–44).

Some people are surprised to discover that this is the only miracle performed by Jesus found in all four Gospels, and with two versions in Matthew and Mark. The fact that we have six versions clearly signals its importance. The Gospel writers tell the story from the ministry of Jesus, something he did in the 30s. But by the time they get around to telling the story some forty to sixty years later, they do so by means of a combination of flashbacks and foreshadowing.

Here's one way to understand it. Imagine that one day in the year 32 Jesus fed 5,000 folks (really more than that, since the number here only included the men) on a hillside in Galilee. Maybe it was a Tuesday. Maybe it was a Wednesday, who knows? Doesn't matter. No one there at the time would have the foggiest idea that in a few short years Jesus would gather his closest followers in an upper room as they ate the Passover meal and tell them to remember him with bread and wine. That's the historical level of the story. But anyone reading one of these Gospel accounts forty years later would have eaten this meal hundreds of times during their lifetime as they remembered Jesus. That's the literary level of the story, what Roland Barthes cleverly refers to as "*deja lu*" (already read).[13] In other words, readers of Mark's gospel would already be familiar with the whole story. So when Mark or any of the others tells about Jesus feeding the multitudes, it was a kind of flashback and foreshadowing at the same time because the verbs of how he *took*, *blessed* (or *gave thanks*), *broke*, and *gave* would have flashed through their minds, resonating with the words of Jesus in that upper room. Here was Jesus offering Eucharist to the masses, a group clearly made up of what scholars call the *Am ha'aretz* (Hebrew for "people of the land"), those living on the edge. It also means that when we read the story of his Last Supper, we are to recall this feeding of the masses. As we will explore later in more detail, Mark's gospel associates the Jesus meal with matters of justice.

But the connections between this feeding narrative and the surrounding ones go even deeper. In the story that follows Jesus makes his disciples get in a boat while he stays behind to pray. The wind is against them, so he comes to them walking on the sea. They mistake him for a ghost, but he calms their fears, telling them not to be afraid. He gets in the boat and the wind stops howling. So far, so good. But then there's a strange twist. At the end of that storm incident, in verse 51 Mark writes, "And they were utterly astounded, for they did not understand about the loaves, but their hearts were hardened." Did you catch it, the connection to the previous story? Mark says they didn't understand about "the loaves." Not, they didn't get his calming the winds, or how storms pop up, but rather they didn't grasp the significance of the "loaves," the lesson of the bread in the previous story. Apparently the feeding story is so crucial that if we get it, we'll get how Jesus can calm winds too. The connection between bread and boats is not readily apparent, I admit.

It could be that Mark wants us to recognize Jesus as Lord of creation. When Jesus comes walking on the water the disciples are understandably frightened until he says, "It is I; do not be afraid" (Mark 6:50). I've always thought of this as an awkward translation for Jesus reassuring them, "It is I." Sounds more like one of the three musketeers than Jesus. The Greek says, "I am." Period. That of course is the name of God in the Old Testament, I AM, a translation of the Hebrew word *Yahweh* (Exodus 3:13–14). Maybe Mark is telling us that Jesus is the I AM, the one who provides food in the wilderness like God did in Israel's history, and who is over the stormy waters as well. No matter how you interpret it, it's clear the disciples hadn't learned anything from Jesus feeding the multitudes.

Even more intriguing is the connection of the feeding story with the one that comes before it. The context is fairly complex, so let me set it up.

King Herod had taken his brother's wife Herodias for himself, something John the Baptizer had been preaching against. Not surprisingly, Herod wasn't thrilled about those kinds of sermons, even if there was something about John's preaching that attracted him. His bride Herodias took it even harder though, not just holding a grudge but wanting to see the prophet of God killed. Here's how the scene unfolds next:

> But an opportunity came when Herod on his birthday gave a banquet for his courtiers and officers and for the leaders of Galilee. When his daughter Herodias came in and danced, she pleased Herod and his guests; and the king said to the girl, "Ask me for whatever you wish, and I will give it." And he solemnly swore to her, "Whatever you ask me, I will give you, even half of my kingdom." She went out and said to her mother, "What should I ask for?" She replied, "The head of John the baptizer." Immediately she rushed back to the king and requested, "I want you to give me at once the head of John the Baptist on a platter." The king was deeply grieved; yet out of regard for his oaths and for the guests, he did not want to refuse her. Immediately the king sent a soldier of the guard with orders to bring John's head. He went and beheaded him in the prison, brought his head on a platter, and gave it to the girl. Then the girl gave it to her mother (Mark 6:21–28).

Such contrasting banquets. Herod's banquet would have occurred in one of his palaces; Jesus' banquet takes place in the wilderness. Herod dines with the elite of Roman society; Jesus feeds the poor and hungry masses. Herod's banquet leads to death; Jesus' banquet leads to life.

In the stories in Luke's gospel we saw that Jesus eats with everyone—toll collectors and Pharisees alike—even if those stories didn't have eucharistic overtones per se. But in this story we see how Mark wants readers to view the feeding of the multitudes as reflecting the church's eucharistic practices. The other three Gospel writers do the very same thing. That means that what we typically call the Last Supper (capital letters) not only wasn't the last one at all since he continued to eat with his followers after the resurrection and still does today; it wasn't the first supper either since Jesus ate so many meals during his ministry, including this one with the multitudes.

It's such a unique way to read the feeding stories, with eucharistic imagery. It reminds me of a church in Atlanta I visited one Sunday a few years back, a large suburban church with auditorium seating and a really loud band. My wife, who is a minister to children in Kansas City, wanted to visit there, see how they have organized their children's ministry. So we worshiped there that morning as well. I knew when the band started that it would not be my cup of tea, so to speak. In high school I listened to Led Zeppelin as loud as anyone, my '68 VW Beetle serving as one big speaker on wheels. But all these years later I'm no longer into loud music, even if some churches now make ear plugs available. Seriously.

The sermon wasn't any better than the loud music. The preacher spoke from the story of Jesus feeding the multitudes, but his message was full of cute stories about himself, about how he took his lunch to school in a paper sack when he was a kid. His treatment of the biblical text did not strike me as particularly deep, interesting, or relevant. I thought, *This is the worst sermon I've ever heard.* Not literally, but you get the idea. I would have given him a C, maybe C+ so as not to hurt his feelings, but it was awful. I tuned him out.

Near the end of his message he had us look under our seats, to reach under there and pull out a small paper sack. *Okay, I'll do it, play along with your little game.* I figured it would be just another stunt. Then he shocked me. He said over the next few weeks that congregation was going to collect food, and the sacks represented the 5,000 families they were going to feed there in the area. Here was the biblical story coming to life. I thought, *This is the best sermon I ever heard. A+.*

One of the most fascinating takes on the feeding of the multitudes is John Dominic Crossan's reflections on that petition about daily bread in the Lord's prayer. He notes how Herod's father had made the village of Sepphoris the capital city, taxing the peasants who farmed the land. Herod, however, came up with a more enterprising scheme, moving the capital to the seaside town of Tiberias where he would not only tax bread but fish as well. If you've ever been to the Holy Land, to the site on the northern shore of the Sea of Galilee where tradition has it Jesus multiplied the bread and fish, you know that it's in plain sight of Herod's capital at Tiberias. According to Crossan, Jesus intends to take back not just the land but the lake for God, and for all of God's people, especially the poor.[14] Read that way, the feeding of the multitudes isn't just the story of a miracle, but a political statement in the face of Herod.

Another scholar suggests how the meals Jesus ate, especially the Passover, were protests against the Roman Empire and its neglect for the poor. Since the Israelites ate the first Passover on the eve of God's delivering them from the Egyptians, similarly the final Passover meal of Jesus would be an indictment against the Romans who occupied the Holy Land.[15] Pharaohs and Caesars have a lot in common, including how they still exist in our day, albeit with different titles.

Near as I can determine, there are only two specific sins associated with this meal in the New Testament, gluttony and neglecting the poor. Not only are the two related as we saw in Paul's letter to Corinth, but Herod, who had been appointed by Rome managed to pull off both. But the Gospels make it clear in the different feeding stories: Jesus will feed the poor, a story with eucharistic inferences, and every one of those six versions include leftovers, signaling there is enough for all. When it comes to this Jesus meal, "It is never just about *food*. It is always about *just* food."[16]

Barbecue Church

The American Royal World Series of Barbecue is a big deal in Kansas City because it's a big deal in lots of places. At this, the largest barbecue contest in the United States, more than 500 teams compete each year in several categories. There are two kinds of judges, and I don't mean fat and fatter, but certified and non-certified. My first time tasting all that barbecue was as someone whose only certification was that I really love barbecue, and the fact that I smoke ribs and pork butt at home from time to time. What kind of training does a person need to decide whether smoked brisket tastes good or not?

My daughter Melissa and I took part, and what a treat. The first year we did it was the first time the event was held at Arrowhead Stadium, where the Kansas City Chiefs normally play. They were playing an away game, so all those barbecue teams filled the parking lot. The nearly 700 judges were seated in groups of six at rectangular tables. We tasted chicken, pulled pork, ribs, brisket, and sausage for more than two hours, six entries in each of the categories. At my table the pulled pork was to die for. We were not hungry when it was over; trust me. I had done something similar two weeks earlier, judging sauces that we dipped pulled pork in for two-plus hours.

Melissa and I were obviously rookies, because even as we were walking in to register, we noticed not just the official T-shirts of the certified judges but the coolers they were carrying. I figured they were smart enough to bring their own beer since the competition only provides bottled water and crackers for cleansing the palate. But no, they were empty coolers because judges take home a lot of meat afterwards. Thankfully, one of the judges at my table gave me some Ziplocs, and I came home with an armful.

Besides a meat coma, several things struck me about the event, especially the ritualistic aspects. I'm a theologian, so I'm always keen to see rituals at work in any context. For instance, we stood and repeated the oath, which began with our acknowledging we know the difference between good barbecue and a McRib sandwich, and which ended with a promise to uphold "truth, justice, and the American way of barbecue." Okay, that's a bit corny, I admit. But standing and raising one's hand is an important moment in any context. I also couldn't help but notice that we were a diverse group, old and young, male and female, black and white, and so forth. And of course there was the fact we had come together over food, really good food. In a way it was "church," and I'm not just saying that to cover my skipping church this particular Sunday morning, World Communion Sunday on top of it. How's that for irony?

Unfortunately, it was like church in one other way. Some of the regulars felt the need to flaunt their sense of belonging and the inexperience of newbies like myself. To be fair, not everyone acted this way. Several of the old hands were welcoming, sharing not just Ziplocs but tips and techniques when smoking meats at home. But for many of them the only way they knew to justify their status was to question ours, thumb their noses in the air. "Oh, this is your first time? This is my thirty-seventh judging." As my son later put it, the judges were apparently good at judging more than barbecue. I have seen something similar in churches.

* * *

As I briefly noted earlier, there were all sorts of clubs and associations (*collegia* in Latin or *ecclesia* in Greek, the latter also being the word translated as "church") in the first-century Mediterranean world, with the Christians borrowing from those as they eventually formed their own identity. Of course as Douglas Boin notes in *Coming Out Christian in the Roman World*, no history can ever be written with definite articles, which we know to be true in our day (*the* Americans, *the* Iranians, *the* Australians, *the* North Koreans) but so easily forget when it comes to people of the past.[17] In this case, we should avoid the term *the* early church, since there were many expressions everywhere and at all times. One thing we do know, to borrow Boin's term, is that Jesus' followers lived "hyphenated lives," Christian and Roman.[18]

The reason this observation is so important as we think about what it means to do and be church today is because of how much even the term *church* has changed since Paul's day. Words like *church* and *worship* in our day have a fairly common meaning, even if the former can refer to a building as well as a group of people. Even so, we clearly do not use these terms the way they did in the first century. An *ecclesia*, the Greek word translated "church," was an assembly. Lots of groups met in such assemblies, and with the kind of banqueting we've been thinking about. Many of these groups were formed because of common interests, men with the same occupation or trade and similar interests in philosophical conversations. Excluding women was fairly common among these groups, especially for the after-dinner conversations.

The various fellowships and associations that we now think of as churches were in some ways more inclusive than society as a whole, and more exclusive too. Here's what I mean. As Wayne Meeks notes, baptism into the faith always implied a "resocialization," with a commitment to the teachings of Jesus and other believers above everything else. If you were going to be part of this Jesus movement, demands would be made on your life, a kind of exclusion. At the same time, Meeks adds, "the Christian groups were much more inclusive in terms of social stratification and other social categories than were the voluntary associations." [19]

Except here's where the picture gets more complicated. Because these gatherings were influenced by the culture in which they lived, status mattered, even as those early Christ followers managed to model more diversity than most other groups. In other words, while there may no longer have been distinctions between "male and female, slave and free," as Paul wrote to the Galatians (Gal 3:28), the pecking order of who sat where was firmly established and some persons didn't get a seat at all.

* * *

One of the fairly well known stories in Luke's gospel is when Jesus goes to a banquet in the home of his close friends Mary and Martha. (This banquet would have followed the same two-part structure, supper and symposium.) As you may recall, Martha is the one "in the kitchen" putting the finishing touches on dinner when not just pots are boiling over but her temper as well. Okay, there's nothing about the pots and a kitchen, but when she confronts Jesus, the language in Greek is quite accusatory: "You really don't care, do you, Lord, that my sister has left me to do all this work?" That's because Mary, who should have been helping her, was in the "living room" with Jesus. I have always appreciated Jesus allowing Mary to be in there with all the men folk, and rightly so. But I have also been troubled by the fact Mary is seated on the floor, some kind of second-class citizen at best (Luke 10:38–42), which was fairly common among groups who let women stick around for the symposium or after-dinner talk. They were insiders, but of a different status, a little lower. Dennis Smith offers another interpretation, that it was mostly "loose" women who reclined at banquets, and that rather than demeaning her or excluding her altogether, Luke has portrayed her as "respectable."[20] (In Mark's feeding story in the wilderness everyone gets to recline at table, so to speak, women and children as well.[21])

While I don't know of any modern congregations that exclude women from the Communion table while the men who are present freely partake, I do know some churches that refuse to let the women serve or preside over the Communion meal, even as they practically insist that the women of the church cook all the meals for potlucks and such. Some things never change.

What I'm wondering about are the ways we claim to be egalitarian in our faith and yet set up boundaries of one sort or another. In some churches little kids can receive a blessing from the pastor while they watch Mom and Dad partake of Communion; but the kids cannot partake. It's one of the few times in their lives that the mother bird eats in front of her little ones and tells them to forget it, they're not getting any. Some people I know claim their earliest childhood memory of this meal is being told no. There is no record of children present at the so-called Last Supper; that is true. Although if there had been, I feel certain Jesus would gladly have fed them. Remember the language of Communion in the wilderness feedings? That meal included women and children.

Sometimes we set up boundaries with the best of intentions, or so I'm told. But they remain boundaries nevertheless. For instance, I was at a church recently where all were invited to feast at the table. Well, sort of *all*. The piece in the bulletin read, "Christ invites to this table all who profess the Christian faith, who endeavor to be at peace with their neighbors, and who seek the mercy of God. All who follow the way of Christ are welcome at this table." A lot of qualifiers accompany the two "all"s in those lines. What if I'm not exactly endeavoring to live in peace with my neighbors but have been calling the cops on them when their parties get out of hand? What if I only partially seek God's mercy? Who exactly is welcome at the table?

* * *

One of the great joys of my life was editing a collection of stories by Fred Craddock. Many ministers and laity alike will recognize his name right away. Craddock was the dean of twentieth-century preaching theory and a great preacher himself, especially known for his homespun storytelling. One of the stories he used to tell is about the first church he ever served, near Oak Ridge, Tennessee. It was a rural congregation, small in numbers as you might expect. Then something happened in that community, namely a large construction project.

A lot of those workers and their families started coming to church, Fred's church. This was so troubling for some of the regulars there that some of the key lay leaders started debating what to do to keep people away. One Sunday after services they convened a meeting, and one of the men made a motion, that unless you were a longtime property owner in that county, you couldn't come to their church. Fred was dumbfounded, spoke against the motion, and moments later it passed. They told him he was still just a young preacher, that this was the right thing to do.

Years later he and his wife Nettie were in that part of the state on a Sunday morning. He wondered whatever had happened to that church, so they decided to find out. The parking lot was packed, cars and trucks, motorcycles too. The sign read, "Barbecue Restaurant."

It was nearly lunchtime, so they figured why not. The pulpit from which he had preached was now in the entry way, with a young girl behind it. "How many in your party?" The table where the congregation had feasted on bread and wine now featured different sauces, pickles, onions, and napkins. Fred and Nettie sat down to eat, and while they were eating, he looked around at the customers there. He said, "You know, it's a good thing this isn't a church any more, or else all these people couldn't be here."[22]

I don't know what your church's gatherings looks like on any given Sunday, especially at the table. I hope the scene is inclusive, not exclusive. I have been imagining a future for us, although this scene could be first century or twenty-first century: all sorts of people arrive with all sorts of dishes. The tall and the short alike bring meats and vegetables. The young and the old alike supply fruits and cheeses. Men and women bring sweets. Gay and straight bring bread and wine. They greet one another with hugs, maybe even a holy kiss on the cheek. They are genuinely glad to see each other. There is small talk about happenings in the city. There is large talk about politics and justice.

They speak words of peace. They tell stories over the meal, including stories about Jesus welcoming even the least. And on this occasion the sign in front of the church tells the truth: all are welcome.

Open Table

I recently went to coffee with two different ministers on two different occasions, the first one introducing me to the second. Nick Pickrell is on staff at Second Presbyterian Church in Kansas City, and they've started a Sunday evening service called The Open Table. You can imagine why the name caught my attention. Nick and I met at this cool place called Crows Coffee, and on the patio talked about all the "dinner church" movements going on around the country, the ones we know about anyway, including how at theirs a truly diverse group of people eat together. Some dinner churches gather mostly church folks who after eating together find other times of the week to feed the poor, like St. Lydia's in New York; others gather the poor around the table with them. The Open Table is in the latter camp. I'll have more to say about The Open Table near the end of this book.

The other minister I had coffee with recently was Tim Suttle, pastor of Redemption Church on the Kansas side of our fair city. Nick had told me about Tim's book that had recently been published, *Shrink*. I ordered the book on Amazon, and a few weeks later I met Tim for coffee at another cool place, Kansas Coffee Company. I've noticed over the last few years how many ministers I know hang out and work in coffee shops. If you're a jealous parishioner, I wouldn't get too upset. Maybe meeting in coffee shops explains in part why more and more clergy are open to different ways of doing church.

Tim's book, *Shrink*, is subtitled *Faithful Ministry in a Church-Growth Culture*.[23] What an honest confession it is, his admitting how he used to be addicted to so-called "success" models touted at conferences that promised to help him grow his congregation or your money back, or some such thing. These conferences were always about growth of the numerical variety. I knew I would like Tim's book because early on he quotes extensively from Wendell Berry's novel, *Jayber Crow*. That's quite the contrast with the number of church growth books that quote from best sellers in business and management principles. In the last twenty years or so, much of the material about church leadership has been more influenced by corporate America than a theological vision of the church.

Suttle invites us to read a scene in Berry's novel where an old farmer Athey Keith and his son-in-law Troy Chatham debate different approaches to farming, except he invites us to substitute the word "church" for "farm." Whereas the elder Athey spoke of caring for the land and the rhythms of life, all young Troy could think was, "We need to plant more corn." (Translated, we need bigger churches and we need to get more people into those churches.) The old man wasn't opposed to production, not at all. He was a farmer, after all; but he wasn't consumed with production at all costs either. Here's just a small excerpt of Athey's response to Troy:

> The law of the farm was in the balance between crops (including hay and pasture) and livestock. The farm would have no more livestock than it could carry without strain. No more land would be plowed for grain crops than could be fertilized with manure from the animals. No more grain would be grown than the animals could eat.[24]

Suttle claims, "What Berry writes about the farm is true of the church." He believes that "tending a farm and tending a church are similar enterprises. After all, they are both the necessary work of the people who have been asked to care for this world."[25] And the church is not about success but faithfulness.

I've preached more than once about God's somewhat peculiar farming techniques, in particular that little parable about that tiny seed, the so-called Mustard Seed parable. In Matthew's version (13:31–32) as well as Luke's (13:18–19), the seed becomes a tree. But in Marks' version (4:30–32), the original version that Matthew and Luke worked from, the seed grows into a bush because that's what mustard seeds become, bushes. One theory is that Jesus' parable in Mark pokes fun at the grand Roman Empire that ruled the Mediterranean world but also Israel's own grand hopes for the coming Messiah. They had always imagined that the coming One would be like the cedars of Lebanon (Ezekiel 17:22–24). Instead, the kingdom (or reign) of God turns out to be more like a bush, albeit still big enough for birds to nest in its shade.[26] Let's face it, in North America we often confuse size and significance.

Tim admits he was once consumed by the "bigger is better" model. He admits he wasn't all that good at it either. But this so-called failure was an epiphany as he came to realize that intimacy often suffers when churches get too big. Tim doesn't quote Will Campbell's line, and I can't remember where I read it, how if a church gets larger than 200, what it needs is not a pastor but a mayor. Suttle now proposes a different church growth strategy, "to get smaller and die." He adds, "I know it is a tough sell, but crucifixion seems like a losing strategy unless you believe in the resurrection."[27]

In my experience, this preoccupation with "bigger is better" appeals mostly to male ministers, not so much females. True, there are women serving large churches, but they don't seem obsessed with it. I recently read an essay suggesting that women tend to be less interested in building a kingdom in the shape of large church plants (the *Father Knows Best* church), but instead are more open to smaller, intimate gatherings, what might be described as "women-shaped communities." In these communities the preaching is often shared, the conversations and visioning open to all voices, and the setting is more oriented to eating around a table.[28] Obviously there are men interested in the dinner church model, but in some ways they have tended to follow the lead of women on this.

Over coffee with Tim I said, "But here's the tricky thing about the 'shrink' movement. If you start a dinner church or some such thing with ten or twelve people committed to sharing life together, others will naturally want to join it. Then the intimacy factor goes out the window." We both knew that was true. How does a congregation welcome everyone in the name of an inclusive God while trying to remain intimate? When I made a similar comment to Emily Scott, founding pastor of Dinner Church in Brooklyn, she said that's why they have a Monday evening option in addition to Sunday, so a different set of people can participate and still keep it intimate. And now they've started Waffle Church, so that families with children can participate more fully at other times of the week.

Turns out, this idea of multiple meetings is an ancient practice, something our ancestors in the faith figured out long ago. First-century banqueting not only included a supper and symposium at which people reclined on couches lining three sides of the room, but formal invitations were also required since there was limited space, typically for nine to twelve persons in all. Think about that, the so-called "church" at Corinth or wherever city was made up of many small clusters throughout that city.

Twice in the last month or so I visited some smaller churches. I was the preacher at one while the minister was away, and just visiting the other on a Sunday I had off. In both cases someone who graciously greeted me promptly began apologizing because their numbers were down that week. These were defensive apologies, the kind that suggest some level of embarrassment, implying "we usually have more people here." That may well be true, but what struck me about this is how we are driven by numbers, absolutely obsessed with them; not just the Dow Jones Industrial in a market-driven world but in the church. Why do we refuse to see the advantages to smaller gatherings?

Plutarch, an ancient authority on banqueting, suggested that the size of gatherings wasn't just determined by space, but decorum. I think another word for "decorum" in this case might be "theology." Plutarch believed the size of a dinner party was right "so long as it easily remains one party. If it gets too large, so that the guests can no longer talk to each other or enjoy the hospitality together or even know one another, then it ceases to be a party at all." Plutarch added it would be worse to "take away the pleasure of conversation at table than to run out of wine,"[29] and running out of wine was a big deal, as the story in John's gospel reminds us (John 2:1–11). Plutarch maintained that even if people were wealthy enough to build a dining room that could hold thirty couches, it would be a mistake, turning the intimate banquet into more of a county fair or a circus. The solution was simple, more frequent banquets and a rotating guest list.[30] Churches could learn from Plutarch's example.

CHAPTER 3

The Ambiance

"Eating with the fullest pleasure . . . we experience and celebrate our
dependence and our gratitude, for we are living from mystery,
from creatures we did not make and powers we cannot comprehend."

—WENDELL BERRY

Festive Joy

In the hilarious indie film *My Big Fat Greek Wedding*, the eccentric father of the bride Gus Portokalos claims that every word comes from the Greek. He says, "Give me a word, any word, and I show you that the root of that word is Greek." According to him, even Japanese words like *kimono* come from the Greek. What a crack-up.

But as we've noted, a lot of our vocabulary does come from the Greek, especially words we use in the life of the church. One of the words you probably won't hear in church, or in seminary for that matter, is *euphrosyne*. Dennis Smith, one of those leading authorities on ancient banqueting, translates the term as "festive joy," the phrase that best summarizes the mood of first-century dinner parties, joy being a gift of the gods and usually associated with wine.[1] Except for the part about many deities, this would have been true for Christian banqueting as well. "Festive joy" seems redundant, I know, since it's hard to imagine a joy that isn't festive or a festiveness without joy. But the Greek word is that explicit, festive joy.

When I was on sabbatical and told people I was writing a book, inevitably someone would ask what it's about. The girl at Starbucks, the public librarian near our house, those golfing buddies in Florida. I don't know that I ever had it down to an "elevator speech," but I would say something about the earliest decades of the Christian movement and how their gatherings were more like a dinner party, the Jesus meal included. Somewhere along the way, I would describe the main traits: full meal that promoted intimacy, mostly inclusive, definitely festive, and with a conversation after the meal that encouraged everyone to participate. It was the festive one that always caught people off guard. "Wait, wait," the person would interrupt, "what do you mean *festive*?" This was the one aspect that intrigued people the most. The fact it was a full meal back then compared to our snack nowadays prompted a mere raising of the eyebrows, even if they craved intimacy and not Styrofoam wafers. How it was mostly inclusive and we have bouncers, okay, that's both sad and interesting. Sermon as after-dinner conversation, that's nice. But when I mentioned that the earliest gatherings were festive, that got their attention. No one person I talked to seemed to be able to get her or his head around this idea: when the earliest church ate this meal, the mood could best be described as festive joy. Think about it: does festive joy best describe the Jesus meal at your church? At any church you know?

Unfortunately, in our day it feels more like a funeral, more like a "baby's funeral." That's how an older unchurched gentleman described a Communion service to a minister friend of mine. A bunch of us clergy were gathered over lunch, decrying the sad state of affairs called Communion, which in many places is exclusively a sad affair, and out comes this statement. "It felt like a baby's funeral." We sat there in stunned silence. It wasn't the first time I had heard Communion compared to a funeral; that's troubling enough. But a *baby's* funeral? Why a baby's funeral? Could it have been the size of the white cloth draped over the bread and chalice, about the size of an infant's limp body? Could it have been the complete ineptness one feels at the death of a child? Whatever the reasoning, such somber words: "It felt like a baby's funeral."

While that comparison came as a complete surprise to me and my minister friends, what did not surprise me was learning that in the New Testament Luke uses that Greek word for festive joy more than anyone else, including three times in the parable of the Father with Two Sons. When the father decides to throw a party, he orders the slaves to kill the fatted calf because this is a special occasion for feasting. He says, "'Let us eat and celebrate; for this son of mine was dead and is alive again; he was lost and is found!' And they began to celebrate" (Luke 15:23–24).[2] The word *celebrate*, used twice here, is the verb form of that Greek word for "festive joy." You could just as easily translate it as, "we had to have fun." I love that idea, the house church's party for wayward children as an occasion of festive joy, a celebration. Apparently, except for the older brother, a fun time was had by all. The word *prodigal*, by the way, which doesn't even occur in this story or anywhere in the Bible, means "extravagant," not rebellious. Some scholars have suggested it's the father who is prodigal, extravagantly throwing a party to celebrate the younger boy's return.

First-century banqueting and the meal we now know as Eucharist were festive occasions, the very life of the party so to speak. Of course religious festivals were supposed to be festive; it's part of the word's etymology. Over time, the church went the opposite direction as we all know, letting so-called secular events be joyful (think watch parties to cheer on the Kansas City Royals in yet another World Series) while sacred ones (think pretty much anything churches do in worship and rituals) would need to be serious, and we all know serious is synonymous with somber.[3] Actually, serious and somber are not the same thing. For instance, you can celebrate your granddad's ninetieth birthday, taking the occasion very seriously, especially in light of his stroke three months earlier, and yet never let the party turn somber. Why be somber? He's alive, for God's sake. Blow out the candles, and let's eat some cake. It's a birthday party, not a funeral.

* * *

I suspect most Protestants would be surprised to learn that the contemporary worship movement got its start with the Catholics. Part of Vatican II in the 1960s, the idea was an emphasis on revitalized worship among other things. All these years later, guitars and drums can be traced to the Vatican. Who knew? But my hunch is that both groups, Protestants as well as Catholics, would be surprised to learn that Vatican II also stressed the idea that Holy Communion be joyful, a celebration. Except while the pope may have influenced the introduction of contemporary worship, things didn't go so well in introducing a joyful Eucharist. Not exactly.

If the beloved Pope Francis were to issue some kind of edict, that from this moment on Communion must be joyful, I don't know if it would make any difference. Catholics and Protestants alike (as well as our Orthodox sisters and brothers), we seem intent on being somber in our religious gatherings. Turns out, it wasn't always easy in the first century either. Even in the Gospels we sense a tension between John the Baptist and Jesus on this very matter. In Luke's foodie Gospel that we looked at earlier, Jesus says, "John the Baptist has come eating no bread and drinking no wine," but of himself he says, "the Son of Man has come eating and drinking, and you say, 'Look, a glutton and a drunkard, a friend of tax collectors and sinners!'" (Luke 7:33–34).

I was thinking about this passage recently when my wife and I attended one of the Third Thursdays at the Nelson-Atkins Museum of Art here in Kansas City. Ever since the new director arrived, things are different at the museum, less staid. When you think about it, museums and churches are often similar in terms of ambiance, quiet places of reverence. Third Thursdays at the Nelson is a new way to think of a museum. The main foyer is transformed into a concert area with live music and happy hour, along with dancers in another gallery and numerous activities happening simultaneously throughout the museum. My wife and I were anxious to experience the trio of classically trained violinists scheduled to play in a little gallery that features among other paintings Caravaggio's *Saint John the Baptist in the Wilderness*.

We sat on one of the benches up front, only a few feet from the trio. The music was lovely, and then at one point I noticed some of the paintings over the shoulders of the musicians. In one of them Abraham appeared to be looking to heaven in sheer delight as he listened in. In another Peter and Paul surrounded Mary and her baby Jesus, all of them taking in the music. We thought it was great. And why not? How can one be somber in the presence of Bach's "Jesu, Joy of Man's Desiring"? It's even got the word *joy* in the title. Well, I guess some people can. Hard as we tried, we could not find a smile on the face of John the Baptist. In the painting he looks down, pensive and serious. As Luke says, he did not come eating bread and drinking wine. Over the centuries that has been the posture of a lot of Christians who have followed his example.

Most every church I know is willing to have ice cream socials in Fellowship Hall, Trunk or Treating in the parking lot at Halloween, summer softball leagues in the park; in other words, festive joy so long as it is not during worship. We seem determined to keep *euphrosyne* out of the sanctuary. Actually, that's not quite true. Most every Sunday we sing joyful songs, smile at the little kids during the children's moment, speak words of joy in a responsive reading. But no matter how joyful the service has been, when it comes time to eat the Jesus meal, no joy.

The Fruit of the Vine

In the late 1990s I was interim minister at a wonderful American Baptist church in the college town of Columbia, Missouri. Columbia's sister city is in Georgia, as in the Republic of Georgia. In 1997 several dignitaries from Kutaisi were in Columbia to foster relations between the two—politicians, journalists, business people, and clergy. There must have been 200 of us in all, groups of ten or so at round tables in the University Center.

Only a handful of Georgians had made the trip, so each table had nine or so of us, and one ambassador from Kutaisi. Apparently part of their job description was to introduce us to Georgian wine, leading a toast or two during the evening. Sounded good to me. Our host uncorked a red wine and poured as we lifted our glasses and drank to our sister cities. It was good wine, that much I remember.

At the end of the evening as folks stood and mingled with those who had been seated at other tables, I compared notes with friends from the church. I said, "I'm not sure I should drive. That was a lot of wine." My friends were surprised. Apparently the other tables had toasted like we had and drank a glass or two. But the host at our table toasted not just once, not twice, or even three times. I said, "I'm pretty sure we toasted everything in both our countries. Our guy toasted air conditioning in the States, the lovely windows in the University Center, maybe even the cheesecake and pattern on the china." I added, "I lost count of the times he said, 'Is this a great country, or what?'" I know I lost track of the bottles we opened and emptied.

What sticks with me from that summer evening all these years later is the warmth we felt for each other. Wine can be a social lubricant, no question, gladdening the human heart, as the psalmist put it (Ps 104:15). Where is that stranger from the other side of the world now? What is he doing? What has happened in his city since then? In ours? For one night we were connected. Wine can do that. It's actually one of the reasons first-century banqueting associated festive joy and wine. A party's success was often judged on how well it promoted joy between those present, and wine helped achieve that, even as drunkenness was discouraged.[4] In his classic book *The Varieties of Religious Experience*, William James extolled alcohol as central to many religions "due to its power to stimulate the mystical faculties of human nature." While there are dangers of drunkenness associated with alcohol, William James called it "the great exciter of the *Yes* function" in us.[5] In her lovely book, *The Spirituality of Wine*, Gisela Kreglinger distinguishes between "severe" and "gentle" intoxication. The latter, she says, "enhances our festive play before God and knows its limitations. It creates a sense of exaltation, jubilation, and gladness."[6]

All these years later some Christians wish Jesus had turned water into grape juice, including I suppose Thomas Bramwell Welch, the Methodist minister turned dentist who opposed alcohol usage and thus invented the pasteurized grape juice still used in many churches today.[7] But that is not how the story in John's gospel goes; it was wine, real wine. I've heard some lame theories over the years how the Greek word indicates a lack of fermentation, or some such thing. Not true. We really should find ways to help our sisters and brothers who battle alcohol addiction without trying to make the ancient biblical texts support our views, and offering Welch's as well as wine is one way we might help.[8] While those earliest Christians drank fermented wine, it is true that most folks in the first century watered it down, both as a way to prevent drunkenness and to keep costs low.

As for the story in John's gospel, here's the basic plot: Jesus and his disciples, and even his mother, attended a wedding in the neighboring village of Cana, not far from Nazareth (John 2:1–11). The problem with the phrase "attended a wedding" is how it conjures up modern day weddings, a Saturday afternoon and evening with the bride's parents spending a small fortune. (This is the voice of experience since both of our daughters were recently married. As for the precise cost, let's not go there.)

First century weddings were over the top in many ways, a highlight in village life, starting with the duration: seven days. You read that right, up to a full week. Everyone in these small villages would put life on hold, no working in the fields or selling in the markets. So it's not surprising that they ran out of wine, but it also meant the reputation of the bride's parents was at stake since they would be publicly shamed. That's when Mary, Jesus' mother, steps in. The exchange between mother and son sounds odd to modern readers. She says, "They have no wine." His response? "Woman, what concern is that to you and to me? My hour has not yet come" (John 2:4).

Mary's turning to Jesus in the first place signals some level of confidence that he can remedy the situation. Had he multiplied baby formula when he was a kid? Not likely. Who knows why? But while Mary is confident in Jesus, he seems on the surface to be perturbed with her, starting with his calling her "Woman." Actually, the exchange is not rude on his part; he simply tells her (and us as readers of the Fourth Gospel) that his time for such things hasn't come yet. What time?

John's gospel is quite different from the first three, the so-called Synoptic Gospels (that phrase means to see things in a similar way, although Matthew, Mark, and Luke are far from identical). John has an entirely unique way of telling the Jesus story, namely in two parts: the book of signs (chapters 1–11) and the book of glory (chapters 12–21). It's not until the latter half that Jesus will openly declare his identity and mission. Before that, the characters on stage and we the readers only get signs, hints that point us toward his true identity. This story is one of those signs.

Mary tells the servants to do whatever he says, and what Jesus says to do is fetch the water jars, six sizable containers capable of holding twenty to thirty gallons each. That's twenty to thirty gallons of *water*. Except as the story unfolds, once the servants fill the jars with good old H2O, the result is 180 gallons of *wine*. If you've been in a wine store, you've no doubt seen those really large bottles sometimes featured, not the standard size. They don't sell bottles even close to what Jesus supplies here. Except this is not just any wine, but the finest vintage according to the steward of the party, "water in excelsis" as Robert Farrar Capon describes it.[9]

But what are we to make of the story? Some scholars believe the interpretive key can be found in the first and last verses. John begins, "On the third day there was a wedding in Cana of Galilee." If you were to read the Fourth Gospel with the calendar app open on your smart phone, you could definitely get confused. Three times prior to this, as Jesus begins his ministry, John writes, "The next day . . ." (John 1:29, 35, 43).[10] So when he tells the wedding story, readers don't really expect it to begin "On the *third* day." But John's not interested in chronology so much as theology. This is a "third day" story (wink, wink), you know, a "third day" story. Even if you didn't make good grades in Sunday school, perhaps you recall what happens in all the Gospels on the third day, when Jesus is raised from the dead.

Following that sort of lead, this wedding story is supposed to signal a great joy to come when God raises Jesus from the dead. Which brings us to the last line of this wedding story, "Jesus did this, the first of his signs, in Cana of Galilee, and revealed his glory; and his disciples believed in him" (John 2:11). There will be seven signs in John's gospel, healings and feedings, that sort of thing, with the last one being the raising of Lazarus (John 11), a kind of foretaste of resurrection as well.

All of that to say, the extravagance of this wedding and wine resonates with the joyous strains of Easter. Jesus is risen! Risen indeed! So it only makes sense that we celebrate when eating in his name and memory.

The Easter Feast

Turns out, the Greek word for festive joy is a neutral term. It means great joy, yes, but not all joys are created equal. True, Luke uses *euphrosyne* in the story of the prodigal, but he also uses it to describe how the rich man lived, the one who ignored the beggar named Lazarus who camped outside the man's door every day. The story begins, "There was a rich man who was dressed in purple and fine linen and who feasted sumptuously every day" (Luke 16:19). His sumptuous feasting is the same word for festive joy. No, not all feasting is created equal. Enjoying a feast, however, isn't the problem; doing so while you ignore the poor right in front of you is.

In her history of "collective joy," *Dancing in the Streets*, Barbara Ehrenreich writes, "While hierarchy is about exclusion, festivity generates inclusiveness. The music invites everyone to the dance; shared food briefly undermines the privilege of class."[11] Recall Paul's concern for the poor among the Corinthian believers we looked at earlier, about how eating the Jesus meal improperly can result in a visit to the emergency room, even the funeral home. I probably shouldn't be so flippant, because clearly for Paul this is serious business. But as we noted earlier, his main concern was justice amidst the community, caring for the least. Unfortunately, a misreading of Paul had led to the somber Lord's Supper services so many of us endure today.

But as much as a misunderstanding of Paul has impacted our worship today, there is an even larger shadow cast over the church's eating preventing us from reveling in festive joy: the crucifixion. In the grand scheme of Christianity, things don't get much bigger than the cross. Its shadow is huge, towering over many a church. After all, Jesus initiates this meal in his remembrance on the "night in which he was betrayed" and when we eat this meal we "proclaim the Lord's death until he comes," according to Paul's account (1 Cor 11:26). You can gild the cross in gold, shine lovely lights on it in a beautiful sanctuary, sing upbeat songs about it, but no matter what you do, the cross hangs heavy over this meal, causing many a worshiper in our day to hang their heads low as they confess their own sins. But is this what Jesus and the writers of his story had in mind for eating in his memory? The answer might surprise you.

Rita Nakashima Brock and Rebecca Ann Parker may not have won a Pulitzer for their book *Saving Paradise*, but the first line of that volume should win some kind of award. "It took Jesus a thousand years to die." Hard to imagine putting a book back on the shelf after reading that sentence. It's a fascinating thought, huh? It took Jesus a thousand years to die. They explain, "Images of his corpse did not appear in churches until the tenth century. Why not?" They figured art historians were mistaken, that the experts had made an error somewhere along the way, so the two women set out to discover the truth on a five-year journey of the Mediterranean world, from catacombs to cathedrals, visiting art museums.

In the sixth-century church St. Apollinare Nuovo, for example, they found "the earliest surviving life story of Jesus depicted in images," twenty-six panels of mosaics, thirteen of them about his life and ministry, the other thirteen about his suffering and resurrection. The first nine panels featured what you might expect in the life of Jesus. Then came panels depicting the end of his life. Panel ten showed Simon of Cyrene carrying the cross for a beleaguered Jesus. But panel eleven did not feature the crucifixion at all; instead, it featured an angel before an empty tomb. Yes, this earliest Christian artwork skipped over the crucifixion! How could that be possible? Brock and Parker leaned in the way the women disciples had leaned into the tomb on that first Easter thousands of years earlier, and the message from the angel was the same, "I know that you are looking for Jesus who was crucified. He is not here" (Matthew 28:5–6). That still gives me goose bumps, seriously.

Having visited church after church in the Mediterranean world, the two women observe that the death of Jesus was "not a key to meaning, not an image of devotion" for his earliest followers. Brock and Parker continue, "The Christ they saw was the incarnate, risen Christ, the child of baptism, the healer of the sick, the teacher of his friends, and the one who defeated death and transfigured the world with the Spirit of life."[12]

So if the crucifixion wasn't primary for those earliest followers, what happened? The history of Christianity is long and complicated of course, but a couple of key moments stand out, both impacting the artwork that was so influential when most folks couldn't read. To this very day these two events continue to shape our theology in ways we hardly even recognize. The first one occurred in the fourth century under Constantine, Emperor of Rome, which I briefly alluded to earlier. He issued an edict, permitting legal status for the Christian cult, eventually converting to Christianity himself and letting the church use public buildings. By the end of that century Christianity would be *the* official religion of the empire and its citizens. We might be tempted to view this as progress, the Christian faith finally being recognized, persecution ended.

Unfortunately, there were many unintended consequences because buildings weren't the only things we inherited. Christianity and the militarism of the Roman Empire became wrapped up in the cross of Jesus. Even though the corpse of Jesus still doesn't show up in artwork in the fourth century, the image of a conquering Jesus does, Constantine conveniently tying war and Christianity together as he fought military battles under the banner of the cross.[13] Various militaries around the world have done so ever since.

The second event took place in the tenth and eleventh centuries, when Christian artwork finally portrayed a crucified Christ, coinciding with the Crusades, a series of military campaigns in our checkered church history. Brock and Parker observe, "Depictions of the crucified Christ proliferated in Europe in the eleventh century and became increasingly grotesque and bloody." In a fashion similar to Mel Gibson's *The Passion of the Christ* that focused on the torture in more detail than any of the Gospels, "New scenes detailed each step of torment—the flogging, the crown of thorns, the nailing to the cross, and the deposition of his body from the cross."[14]

A focus on the cross and Jesus' bloody death slowly but surely replaced what had been a focus on the goodness of creation and the resurrection of Jesus. I noted earlier that in the grand scheme of Christianity things don't get much bigger than crucifixion. That's true, but there is one thing bigger, the resurrection. The resurrection of Jesus overshadows the cross. Or it's supposed to.

To be sure, those earliest followers of Jesus did not ignore the cross. Not hardly. Every year during Holy Week they remembered the crucifixion specifically, eating the meal with a measured solemnity on Thursday and/or Friday prior to Easter. But that was only one week of the year, not every Sunday. Here's one way to think about what we have done to this meal, something of another historical development, and a cultural one too. Ask someone how many days there are in Lent, and you're likely to hear, "Forty." That's right in a way, but not the whole story. If you look on any Hallmark calendar, the stretch from Ash Wednesday to Easter Sunday is forty-six days long, not forty. That's because the six Sundays are not part of the tally, Sunday being the day of resurrection. Sundays aren't supposed to count in that solemn season. And since Lent is a time of solemn introspection, of fasting not only from food in some traditions but even from saying Alleluia, then Sundays can't be somber, even in Lent. But, and here's the catch, because congregations today may not even see each other during the week, we cram the forty days of Lent into the six Sundays and thus the day of resurrection becomes somber each spring. In some ways Lent is only six days for many Christians today.

Something similar happens with the Jesus meal. Those earliest followers of Jesus ate with festive joy, but not during Holy Week, the one time a year when the meal was somber. Laurence Hull Stookey, a leading authority on church worship, claims that for centuries we have outright ignored the joy. "The Supper of the Lord has been a kind of perpetual Holy Thursday evening inserted awkwardly and infrequently into the Sunday morning schedule."[15] Sure, our Holy Week times of worship are somber, eating this meal as we recall the death of Jesus; but that is not the final word. Yet for reasons hard to explain, the church has imported the mood of the Last Supper onto every Sunday's Lord's Supper. Why should the church be sad when eating a meal in remembrance of the resurrected Jesus? Those are joyous strains. In our day even funerals have become more celebrations of life than exclusively somber affairs, and that's for someone who has died. Jesus died, yes, but that wasn't the final word.

The French have a word for food that tastes like the place it was raised, *terroir*. The best wines and cheeses are said to have the soil of the place inside them.[16] Some wine makers claim there is a taste even in the land's rocks. Personally, I'd rather drink the wine than lick the rocks, but the notion of *terroir* got me to thinking. What is the place of the bread and wine we eat in Jesus' name? Most of us grew up thinking exclusively about an upper room and pending death, but it seems to me there are many places in the Gospels besides just an upper room, including those stories of Jesus feasting, especially in light of the resurrection.

A Meal Called Forgiveness

My first Communion, as it were, happened when I was nineteen years old. Having long left the Catholic faith of my childhood behind—choosing to sleep in, or watch TV, or later in my high school days to recover from a raucous Saturday night—I didn't go to church again until the spring semester of my freshman year in college. So shallow was the soil of my young soul, when I graduated from high school my life's ambition was to grow my hair long. And to make a lot of money. I'm not sure how the money part was supposed to happen since growing my hair long took up most of my energy, that and partying. So when Teri, a young lady in all five of my college classes, told me about Jesus, nobody was more surprised than me that the seeds planted took root. Out carousing with my best friend Dennis, I pulled up at the curb in front of his house late one Saturday. Before he rolled out of the car and stumbled up his driveway, I blurted out, "Hey, you want to go to church tomorrow?" Never have more unexpected words come from my mouth. I won't print his response here, but it starts with an F and translates as no!

What is even crazier is that I managed to get up in time the next morning to attend a church. I'm pretty sure it was Easter Sunday because while I don't remember much about the day, I do recall a lot of ladies in hats which really wasn't the norm in the late '70s except on Easter. I attended another church the following Sunday, then finally the week after that met Teri at her church. This was the Sunday when that baptism in St. Christopher's Catholic Church nineteen years earlier finally took hold.

After that, I started attending the college and career class during Sunday school, and sitting with my new friends in worship. While I sang "Amazing Grace" on Sundays, the stereo in my '68 Beetle still blared with ZZ Top or Eric Clapton before and after services. On a more serious level, I was still partying, or so I seem to recall because one Sunday when I plopped down in the pew, I looked up horrified to see those trays on the Lord's table. This was Communion Sunday, a once a month thing in that congregation. *Just my luck*, I thought. If I could have snuck out of the service or squeezed underneath the pew, I would have. I felt like crap, and that was my first Communion.

As you might imagine, I'm not drawn to this sort of eucharistic service, worshipers wallowing in guilt and shame as they eat this meal. What kind of dinner party is that? Along with a misreading of Paul, fixating on the Last Supper in the upper room could easily lead to such a practice. I'm fairly certain that most of the time we're not confessing gluttony or how we have forsaken the poor, but something else entirely. Whatever sins any of us may have committed, we come to the table forgiven by God.

That said there is another story in the Gospels about a meal and for-giveness, a story so beautiful it should not be omitted. It's the last story John tells in his recounting of the Jesus story. If you've ever read the Fourth Gospel closely, you know it features two endings. Chapter twenty is about the resurrection of Jesus, and that chapter ends with a line about how Jesus "did many other signs in the presence of his disciples, which are not writ-ten in this book" (John 20:30). The end, right? Not exactly, because shortly after putting his pen down, he picks it back up and tells one more story in chapter 21. Thank God. This is how it goes:

Peter, the ringleader of the disciples, announces he is going fishing. That seems innocent enough, except the way it is described you get the idea it involved more than catching fish. He and several of the disciples had been fishermen before Jesus called them to follow him. Now Peter and some of the others return to the waters. There is a kind of resignation to this trip. I say that because not only does John tell us how that night they caught nothing, but this is the first personal encounter Jesus will have with Peter after he denied his Lord three times.

While they are fishing, Jesus appears on the shore and asks, "Chil-dren, you don't have any fish, do you?" That doesn't seem very kind, call-ing them kids and teasing them about no catch. Jesus tells them to cast their net again, and when they do, the catch is overwhelming. Peter, real-izing it's Jesus, jumps in the water and swims ashore. I wonder if halfway there he had second thoughts. Remember, the last time Peter was on stage in John's gospel drama was in the courtyard of the high priest, Jesus go-ing to trial. On three occasions there in that courtyard Peter denied even knowing Jesus, which is of course what Jesus had predicted in the upper room (John 13:36–38).

So I imagine that what started off as a Michael Phelps freestyle sprint to the beach may have turned to a slow breaststroke or dog paddle as he recalled his betrayal. When Peter finally gets there, Jesus has prepared breakfast, some fish on a charcoal fire. This is one of those moments where reading all the way through John's gospel in one sitting would really help. Or if Steven Spielberg did a cinematic version, it would be much clearer to us. The scene of Peter's betrayal in the courtyard took place around a char-coal fire, and now here we are again around such a fire. The camera would focus on one fire, then the other, with one of those clever Hollywood edits.

If that weren't enough, the threefold denial now leads to a threefold questioning, Jesus asking Peter, "Do you love me?" Three times! And each time he asks, Peter responds, "Yes, Lord, you know that I love you." And each time Peter confesses his love, Jesus reminds Peter that he has been called to "feed my lambs."

I suppose the only thing that would make this story any better, and it's a great story already, is if John had used eucharistic language, Jesus taking, blessing, and so forth. But it's still a classic moment, a meal of fish with a side order of grace.

I have always been drawn to this story, in part because of the threefold questioning, but perhaps even more so because of the tenderness. Peter and the others catch nothing, a very telling indicator of life without Christ. And instead of a scolding or humiliation, Jesus offers a meal and forgiveness. So long as our Communion meals can help people to know forgiveness and not humiliation and shame, we should be eating with great joy. One of the good practices in many of our churches is a time of confession and pardon prior to eating the Jesus meal. This story in John also reminds me of that closing scene in the movie *Places in the Heart*. If you haven't seen it, check it out, although the closing scene only makes sense in light of the film's opening scene; so watch the whole thing.

Whenever I have preached from this story in John's gospel, I have recalled something that happened to me years ago now. We had a student named Joe graduate from the seminary where I then taught. He went to a church in Newark, Ohio. For his installation service he invited my New Testament colleague, David May, and me to be part of the weekend. And we made a weekend of it. On Friday night David and I led a Bible study on word and table, what happens in the church's preaching and at table every week. Saturday morning we had a little golf outing. On Saturday evening would be the installation and ordination service, and on Sunday morning, the newly installed pastor would preach his first sermon there.

David and I dropped by Joe's house on Saturday afternoon, a couple of hours prior to the service that evening. Understandably, Joe had lots of extended family in town, so it caught us off guard when we were informed that we were all going out to eat on the way to church that evening. David and I looked at our watches, trying to figure out how nineteen of us were going to get into a restaurant and out in time to get to the church. I mean, it's not like we could be a little late or something. So we suggested the two of us would go ahead to the restaurant and put our name on the waiting list.

They had decided on this lovely place that specialized in home cooking, a restaurant owned by an Amish family, Miller's. The place was packed. In the waiting area they sold Longaberger baskets to those willing to take out a second mortgage on their homes, and they had a bakery with freshly baked breads, jams, and apple butter for sale as well. It made your mouth water while you waited for your table. And waiting for your table was definitely the norm. I wiggled through the folks, made my way to the front, where the Amish man stood behind an old pulpit and took down names and the size of your party. Beside him was a young Amish girl, maybe his daughter, with the cotton dress, and a little hat on her head. The wood-carved sign next to them read, "Please do not give your name until everyone in your party is present." I understood why, but I also knew how long it would take for a table for nineteen to be ready. So I said, "Yes, the name is Graves, party of nineteen." Then the Amish man with the little beard looked me in the eye and said, "And is your whole party present?" Haltingly but somewhat convincingly I said, "Yes."

I know, I know, I lied. It wasn't like I was trying to beat the system. It looked to me like most small parties were waiting the better part of thirty minutes, so it didn't seem like that big of a deal. I found David, who had seen the sign too. He said, "You lied to the Amish? You shouldn't lie to the Amish. The Amish?" I said, "I know, but Joe and his family are on their way and by the time they call our name, they'll be here." Two minutes later came the announcement, "Graves, party of nineteen." I couldn't believe it. David said, "I told you not to lie to the Amish." I told him to shut up and go see if they were pulling into the parking lot. They weren't. I said to call Joe and his family and see where they were. He called. Joe said they were having trouble. I thought, *They're having trouble? You should see my situation.*

I wiggled my way back to the pulpit, bringing David with me. Strength in numbers. There was the young Amish girl with the cotton dress. Beside her, the Amish man with the kind bearded face. At least I hoped it was kind. Beside them both was that darn sign. I said, "Yes, the Graves party, well, uh, I guess we're not all quite here yet." I may have giggled a little too. He looked me in the eye and asked matter-of-factly, "Did you lie?" Dead silence all around. It was like we were in church. The people immediately around us were wide-eyed and wondering. I replied softly, "Yes, I lied." He said rather forcefully, "You two, come with me." I couldn't imagine what he was going to do. What kind of punishment do the Amish hand out to liars? I pictured stocks, or caning, some kind of penance. We followed him through the restaurant, and I thought maybe I was going to make a public confession. But he kept on leading us toward the back, where I thought maybe he would throw us out.

Instead, he opened the door to a large banquet room, a long table set with bread and jams. He offered a gentle smile and said, "Have some bread. You are forgiven."

The Last Word

In his quirky little book, *Party Spirit*, Robert Farrar Capon claims that when hosting a party, it's important we sit down fifteen minutes before everyone arrives and pour ourselves a glass of wine while listening to Vivaldi. Why? Shouldn't we be scurrying around, putting the finishing touches together? Not according to Capon. He says it's because a party is an act of faith; it's going to happen even if we sit on our duffs. We send out invitations ahead of time, signaling we think this future gathering will actually come about. Capon compares this to how the Bible itself ends, with a banquet in heaven (Rev 19). The Bible ends with a party scene because that is our future.[17]

If the death of Jesus isn't the final word, neither is resurrection. Not really. The resurrection overshadows death, but there is at least one other reason for festive joy when eating in Jesus' name: *parousia*. Yes, another Greek word, this one the term for his second coming or return. In Luke's account Jesus tells his disciples he won't be eating this meal again until "it is fulfilled in the kingdom of God" (Luke 22:14–16). Even Paul emphasizes *parousia* when he writes that we eat this meal "until he comes" (1 Cor 11:26). As one scholar notes, after Jesus' ascension to heaven, "the church is found mostly feasting rather than fasting . . . . To fast or feast reveals whether a person awaits the kingdom or participates in it already."[18]

Of course, this waiting is a two-sided coin. True, we eat in joy because one day we will all sit at a huge table, enjoying the heavenly banquet. But note the phrase *one day*. Not yet, not now. Sometime in the future. As André Resner notes in his book *Living In-Between*, the Apostles' Creed declares that Jesus ascended to heaven, and now sits on God's right hand, and from there he will come again, but that's still future tense. Resner writes, "What the ?!#@%! I say, come on, God, get on with it! Finish what you started, already! The early church said, 'Maranatha, come Lord Jesus!' They meant the same thing."[19]

In Jewish tradition one of the images of the world to come is a huge grape: "There will be no grape that will not contain thirty kegs of wine."[20] But right now that grape appears to have been mushed on the way home from the grocery store, heavy canned goods squishing our produce. How do we eat with festive joy in a world that groans, the weight of sin heavy on us all, even creation? Did those first-century Christians just pretend life under Roman rule wasn't that bad? "Here, have another glass of wine. That should take the sting off." Obviously not. As the theologian Jürgen Moltmann rightly reminds us, the joy of life is not *produced* by our feasting together; the banquet is a *demonstration* of a joy that comes from being grounded in God.[21] That sentence is worth reading again because this is a crucial distinction when feasting on the Jesus meal.

* * *

For more than seven years my mom battled Alzheimer's, her memory slipping but not her love for chocolate. When I learned that Greek word for festive joy, I thought it was the perfect term to describe my mother with chocolate. Chocolate milkshakes, chocolate chip cookies, chocolate candy bars, my homemade chocolate cheesecake. I didn't need a Greek dictionary to understand *euphrosyne*; I could just watch her with a carton of Whoppers, those chocolate candies.

We moved her from Texas to Missouri when she was first diagnosed, since I'm the only child and she would need care, starting with someone to drive her to the store each week. When she began to lose her vocabulary, grocery shopping became a game we played together, the two of us standing in the aisle while I guessed what else she might need. Whoppers were always on the list. So I was surprised when one day she said no, she was trying to quit eating so much chocolate. A few minutes later she promptly placed three cartons of Whoppers in her basket. When I said, "I thought you were trying to quit eating so much chocolate." She replied, "I said I'm *trying* to quit. I'm not *quitting*." Never have I laughed so hard in a grocery store.

And never have I cried so hard as when my mom began to slip away. The woman loved food, not just chocolate. She was especially fond of junk food, but also cranberry Jell-O salad at Thanksgiving and my wife's homemade rolls. My mom loved a hamburger and fries, too. When she passed, my good friend Jim Gordon did the service and afterwards we had a wonderful meal in her honor.

How does the church eat with festive joy when life is crashing in? Although not writing specifically about this meal, André Resner asks, "What fills the space between Jesus' first and second comings into this world?" A lot of things of course. He continues, "On one side of the globe a family vacationing on pure white beaches schedules an afternoon of snorkeling amid startlingly beautiful reefs. On the other side of the world, women and girls are divided from the men and boys in their families at gunpoint. The men are summarily murdered. The women are catalogued and sold into the sex slavery market."[22]

Mark it down, if you gather with a small group of friends for some version of dinner church, pains will emerge, learning about aging parents with Alzheimer's. Honestly, this caught me off guard, the vulnerability of small groups. That small group that got together at our house to study early meal practices and then had an Italian dinner/agape feast was no exception. Or there was another group of friends who went on a retreat together down in the Ozarks. Yes, we had a wonderful time and good food, but the pains emerged. This is not a profound insight, I realize, but one worth recalling: everyone you and I know is either facing a crisis themselves or in their immediate circle of family and friends. Alzheimer's, cancer, depression, miscarriage, addiction, the list never ends. And if you sign up to be part of a small group, there's not enough Pinot Grigio in the world to hide the pain.

How, then, shall we feast? Quite often, with heavy hearts. But not without hope. In one of Paul's most beautiful passages, he confesses, "We are afflicted in every way, but not crushed" (2 Cor 4:8). When I had my eucharistic epiphany all those years ago down in Arkansas, it was a vision of broken people coming to eat broken bread, all in hopes of being made whole. This kind of pain is part of this meal even if not central. As a scholar friend recently reminded me, the Black Lives Matter movement has been accompanied by the Black Joy movement as well because celebrating in the face of evil is another form of protest, a way to say that what is wrong in the world will not have the last word, not even now. My friend quoted the title of Alice Walker's collection of poetry, *Hard Times Require Furious Dancing*.[23]

I have always found comfort in an image from the theologian Alan Lewis, who claims that as Christians we reside in Holy Saturday, with one foot in the despair of Good Friday and the other in the resurrection joy of Easter, neither story drowning out the other entirely. Lewis's work bears witness to both truths, written as it was while he battled cancer. It was a battle he lost but not without the hope of the resurrection.[24]

Sure, I'd love to drink wine tonight and not hear about your daughter's diagnosis or your dad's stroke. I'd like to pretend just for one evening there are no wars in this world, no famines, no abductions of a village's young girls. But that's not going to happen no matter how much wine and food we have. Will there be times when the festive joy is tempered? Absolutely. Why do we eat after funerals if not as a foretaste of the heavenly banquet to come?

* * *

Several years ago my best friend and New Testament scholar, David May, and I led a trip to the Holy Land, thirty-eight pilgrims, returning with only thirty-seven, which is not how such trips are supposed to go. We've led several trips since, but something went horribly wrong on this first one. We started in the northern coastal city of Caesarea Maritima and wound our way down through the Jordan Valley, the route most common among tour groups. The ruins at Beth Shean are impressive, an ancient Roman city with bathhouses and a coliseum on paved streets. That's where Herman, a retired physician there with his wife, Mary, went missing. She said she couldn't find him, so while all the others loaded on to the bus, David and I confidently hunted, knowing that we would find him in a matter of minutes and we would be on our way again.

Except we didn't find him. Not that Friday, or for the next several days. Mary and I stayed behind for two days while the rest of our group headed to Jerusalem. Mary and I spent our time with park officials, the local police, military personnel, and Israeli intelligence. We watched riders on horseback comb the area, along with search dogs, helicopters, even airplanes; and in the dark we watched them use infrared devices to see if they could find him. Nothing. Herman had somehow disappeared. The authorities encouraged us to rejoin our group, that they would contact us immediately if something developed.

Mary and I eventually joined the rest of them in Jerusalem, the city of God. Only instead of touring that Sunday morning, Pentecost Sunday, we took a walk. Later that morning we met up with an old physician friend of Herm's, Leon Roski, who lives in Tel Aviv. He and his grown daughter came to the hotel. The daughter personally made posters with Herm's picture and went through the streets of Beth Shean to help with the search. Forty years earlier, it was Herm who delivered her into this world, and now she hoped to return the favor and deliver him.

By Tuesday, Herm had been missing for four days and we wondered what chances there were for good news. That day we went with the group into the Old City of Jerusalem, walking the Via Delarosa, the way of suffering. Legend has it this is the route Jesus took on his way to the cross, and it's the place where pilgrims also remember the sufferings of another woman named Mary. And it was there we got the phone call that Herm's body had been found, apparently dead from heat stroke and dehydration. We cried together, then the others on the trip encircled Mary before she and I headed back to identify the body.

Earlier on the Friday when he went missing, the sun was setting and Sabbath beginning. The Israeli authorities assured us that it would not derail their efforts because nothing is more important than human life. We were sad, or maybe numb is a better way to say it. But Sabbath in Jewish life is a time to celebrate, so while for lunch the police had provided boxed meals, during Sabbath they prepared a delicious soup that Iraqi Jews brought back to Israel in the late 1940s. Mary even thought to ask for the recipe. We ate by candlelight, and it was a brief moment of respite.

It is a strange thing to eat a feast at such a time, but what observant Jews know is that even in suffering, God's good gifts of food and wine are to be enjoyed. These are a people who have known the Holocaust, and who still feast. This festive joy that our ancestors practiced is not the same as a pep rally, but this much I know, the Jesus meal is not a funeral without hope.

Celebrating at the Table

I want to buy you a glass of wine, or ice tea if you prefer. If you will let me, I want to hear your story, the good, bad, and even the ugly. I want to share my story as well, about the indescribable joy of our granddaughter, Emma, who is growing so quickly, and now has a little sister, Olivia. I also want to tell you about losing my parents only three weeks apart, both to Alzheimer's, and that shortly after Emma's birth. But I also want to order us some garlic bread because gathering over food is a celebration. Let us celebrate the goodness of God as we eat and drink. I want to offer a Jewish toast, "L'Chaim," to life, the good and the not so good.

Friends do similar things all the time, all across the world. You can sit in a bistro or pub and watch them. That's a form of education in itself. What if church looked more like that? What does the ambiance of festive joy look like during a worship service? What sorts of things might we do to make it more festive? I made this my mission of late, and I'm happy to report with a fair amount of success. The pastors who invited me to preach for them in conventional worship services were more than accommodating when I suggested a Communion service with a twist of festive joy. So take another bite of bread and a drink while I tell you about some of those experiences.

One of my favorite words in my Introduction to Worship class is *catechesis*. Not the class young people take before baptism, learning an ancient catechism. I'm thinking more about James K. A. Smith's insistence that if people are going to enter into worship more fully, they will need to understand what's happening, and his term for that is *catechesis*.[25] He is so right.

I tell my students that the people in most worship services have little to no appreciation for why we do what we do. Why did the worship team place that song after that Scripture reading? Why do we have silence during a time of confession? Why do we pass the peace, greet one another? Why does this follow that?

Applied to the Jesus meal, why do we call it what we call it? How many churchgoers know the difference between Communion and Eucharist? I found that if I wanted a congregation to enter into a joyful Eucharist, I couldn't just expect joy on their parts or conjure it up. "Come on, folks, look happy. You can do it. Smile!" No, that simply won't work. The sermon I preached would need to set the tone, serving as catechesis, teaching people the nature of this banquet in Jesus' name. So if your church is going to celebrate a joyful meal together, that's where I would start, the teaching and preaching ministry of your congregation. If you're not the preacher, talk to your pastor about these ideas. Invite her/him to read this book with you. If you're in a small group, study this meal together.

Of course we all know that one of the strongest influences on the ambiance of worship is music. Scour the hymnal of your own tradition, the section with songs for Communion, and what you're likely to find are mostly dirges, sad and heavy songs, contemplative in nature, and with a bent toward somberness. Finding a festive hymn for the Eucharist is like looking for Waldo; he's in the picture somewhere, but where?

In my own Disciples of Christ tradition, we have the *Chalice Hymnal*, a chalice being the official icon of the denomination. And because we are a people who eat the Jesus meal each week, we have a good selection of hymns in a section titled "The Church at Worship: The Lord's Supper." When I say a good selection, I mean forty different hymns, which seems like a whole lot more than most hymnals I've seen. Full disclosure, I am not a musician, and somehow even those words don't do justice to how inadequate my music abilities are. But I can read a time signature and recognize the difference between sharps and flats, that sort of thing. What anyone can recognize, musician or not, are minor keys, hymns that in tune and text are intended to respect the solemnity of the Lord's Supper.

Rather than catalog the somber ones, let me share the joyful ones with you. Using YouTube and calling upon some of my musician friends, near as I call tell, we have about ten out of the forty that are joyful to some degree. These include: "We Come as Guests Invited," "One Bread, One Body," "Seed, Scattered and Sown," "In Remembrance of Me," "A Hymn of Joy We Sing," "Come, Share the Lord," "Take Our Bread," "All Who Hunger Gather Gladly," "I Come with Joy," "Let Us Talents and Tongues Employ," and "I'm Gonna Eat at the Welcome Table." I guess one in every four is pretty good, but considering how this meal was originally festive, three out of every four being somber doesn't feel like something we should brag about. Seems to me the percentages should be reversed.

Of course it's tricky cataloging joyful vs. somber. Some solemn Lord's Supper hymns can be sung to more upbeat tunes than the ones in the various hymnals, and some joyful tunes come with somber lyrics. Finding a hymn that is joyful in lyrics and tune, that's a little harder, although they are out there. Like I said, try YouTube. That's where I found different arrangements for the different hymns. As for the lyrics themselves, you don't really need a degree. It's obvious whether it's a hymn of festive joy or more fitting for Maundy Thursday.

Even with all that festive joy at those first-century banquets, there were social protocols that also needed to be followed, or to put it in the colloquial, no one was supposed to end up with a lampshade on their heads. In order to preserve some sort of decency and order (and here my Presbyterians friends are no doubt smiling), a *symposiarch* was appointed, literally "leader of the symposium." In secular banquets, this person might be voted on at the beginning of the evening, with duties including how much water to mix with the wine and arranging the entertainment.[26] In the life of Christ followers, when people like Paul were present, he would be in charge, making sure things didn't get out of hand. Our churches need to follow his lead.

* * *

One of the first festive celebrations I ever led was years ago when I was the featured preacher for the Fellowship of American Baptist Musicians, something I've been honored to do twice now. I may not *be* a musician, but I *love* music and musicians. So preaching in those services with all those talented people was a real gift. I did a similar thing for the Association of Disciples Musicians more recently. The first time with those American Baptists was at their conference center in Green Lake, Wisconsin, which also happens to have two eighteen-hole golf courses. Worship and golf, good stuff.

The people in charge of the week not only asked me to preach every morning but to lead two workshops, one biblical in nature (we looked at the parables of Jesus) and the other more topical but focused on some aspect of worship (we considered the Jesus meal). I told the twenty or so musicians in my Lord's Supper workshop that I had one mission in mind. They knew better than I that the tradition for Friday's service was to conclude the week with a Lord's Supper service down by the lake. They also knew that such services were rarely joyful, so our mission was to transform the somber into joy, and I figured their help would be essential. I think we pulled it off because my workshop participants were in on the planning, and because of the hymns we chose. We sang eucharistic hymns of an upbeat nature, and even when worshipers came forward to eat the bread and dip it in the cup, we had a jazz ensemble playing. Words cannot describe the joy that spilled over by that lake.

There was one other thing we did, something I've copied ever since in more traditional settings too. We passed the peace while people were feasting. It's such a simple thing, but it really works. Now if you're part of a tradition that doesn't pass the peace, I'm guessing you do something similar, even if you call it "Greeting Your Neighbors" or some such thing. In some traditions, worshipers are discouraged from saying anything other than, "Peace be with you," to which the other person responds, "And also with you." In other traditions, it might be small talk about the grandkids or even sports. Call it what you want, that's what we did while they were eating; we greeted one another and fellowshipped.

I even did something similar recently at a church a couple of hours south of Kansas City, First Community Church in Joplin, Missouri, a congregation that passes the trays of bread and little cups. Honestly, I wasn't sure it would work while passing trays. The congregants remained standing instead of their usual practice of sitting, passing the trays while visiting, eating the bread and holding the cup until we all feasted together. They told their minister afterwards this should be the pattern every Sunday, and so that's what they've done every Sunday since.

On one occasion at Second Baptist Church in Liberty, a suburb of Kansas City, they were fine with coming forward, although some were reluctant about a festive atmosphere. I decided I wouldn't be a server at one of the stations but would float around the sanctuary. I wanted to feel what they were feeling, hear what they were saying to each other. And I have to say, it's an incredible experience, even in a grand old sanctuary. Sure, dinner church or some variant around dinner tables is ideal, but the most reserved congregations where I've been become joyful, even boisterous, as they feast together. The Greek word is *euphrosyne*. I don't know what the English would be. Great fun, maybe? Actually, if we translated the verb into a noun, I guess it would be a "celebration."

* * *

I realize that for some churchgoers, great fun is fine, even in the sanctuary from time to time, so long as it's a skit by the youth group, about their upcoming mission trip. Or the little children are singing, and well, they're just so cute, and who cares if that one girl Tabitha has hiked up her dress and little Eric is exploring the Communion table. But joy *during* Communion, that's a different story. When my minister friend Glen and I went to lunch some time back, catching up and talking shop (a supper and symposium if ever there was one), I described what I think a joyful Eucharist looks like. He said the last time he tried it, most folks loved it, but there were some who complained, noting how he had ruined their private time of devotion. I don't remember what he said in response to that.

I know what I would say, or at least like to say, although I'd probably have to find a nicer way to say it, but "too bad, so sad," because Communion is not intended to be a time of personal devotion. Just recently I was invited back to Second Baptist Church in the suburbs of Kansas City where I had preached about a joyful Eucharist six months earlier, this time to lead a four-week study on the subject. The associate pastor who invited me said folks were still talking about that festive Sunday last summer. Since this was a midweek study, there was a soup and salad supper just prior to the sessions themselves. Over supper one evening I was seated by a woman who admitted that while she found the joyful Eucharist fascinating, it was a little out of her comfort zone. When I pressed her to say more, she shared it wasn't that she's an introvert and how that much camaraderie and visiting got under her skin. No, for her Communion is a time of personal reflection, a time to be thankful and quiet before God.

I listened to her views and she listened to mine, which over dinner constitutes yet another form of supper and symposium. As I have reflected on what she said, I wonder if there aren't more appropriate times in the typical worship service for quiet reflection and meditation. I've always told my students in the Intro to Worship course how silence is an endangered species in church services these days. The fact is that the church has developed the notion of a quiet and reflective Communion, when it was originally a festive dinner party. Communion happens in the plural, not singular. The concept of the *individual self* didn't even exist the way it does now until as recently as the sixteenth century.[27] Sure, we commune with God but also with those around us.

I have also encountered some church folks along the way who are opposed to celebrations, period. Maybe not "period," but "semi-colon" for sure. They have no problem with a joyful celebration of their anniversary or a birthday, but when it comes to church, celebrations simply do not belong. Such ascetic thinking reminds me of Robyn Cadwallader's novel *The Anchoress*. It's the story of a woman named Sarah, who at the age of seventeen decides to avoid an arranged marriage, become a nun and more than that, an anchoress. That's not a common term for most of us, referring to someone who not only led a monastic lifestyle but who was actually shut away from all of life in a small dark cell. As she quickly discovers, even walls can't keep out everything. There are sensual longings that she has denied, and keeps trying to deny. There's also the smell of food that "crept in through gaps in the shutters and lingered around me," observes Sarah. She had heard rumors that the anchoress before her had survived on only Communion bread. On one particular fall day she could overhear the sounds of Friaston Market, where she recalled pies, "the smell thick and rich," or "steaming baked apples, the skin tough and tart, the quick burn then the fluff of sweet flesh, sharp spices weaving flavors in my mouth."[28]

Cadwallader later describes the eating of another apple with such sensuality, I was reminded of Meg Ryan's moaning in *When Harry Met Sally*. Some artists have a gift for describing the sensual, and all of us are wired to respond. But when it comes to things holy, like church and Communion, we deny ourselves, try to lock ourselves away. What a pity.

There is a lovely thought in Judaism, a line from the rabbis about how in the world to come God will ask, "Did you enjoy my world?" Good question. The Jesus meal offers a great opportunity for feasting in joy.

CHAPTER 4

The Conversation

"God is capable of all speech acts except that of monologue."

—George Steiner

Participation

It's not every day someone reflects on what an eighteenth-century philosopher had to say about anything, especially thoughts about worship by someone who lived in Denmark. But Søren Kierkegaard's impact on Christian thinking has been substantial even if you've never heard of him. He was painfully aware that his fellow Danes claimed to live in a Christian society, but he didn't see much evidence of that, so he tried to figure out a strategy for communicating faith to people who thought they already possessed it. What he came up with was parables, much like Jesus had centuries earlier. Parables invite us into the world of stories, and at the same time parables sneak up on us with truths we might not have considered otherwise.

For instance, Kierkegaard told one parable called "The Domestic Goose," about a village where only geese lived. Each Sunday in this village all the geese waddled down the road to attend goose church, where they listened to the geese choir and the gander preacher. Pretty much every Sunday the preacher would proclaim, "We are geese." No one got too excited, but one Sunday the goose preacher said with even more force, "No, we are geese, and geese can fly. We were meant to fly." Well, the goose preacher got everyone to thinking and there was even an "amen" from the geese congregation. Geese are meant to fly; this would change everything. After church was over, they all waddled back home.[1] Ouch.

Kierkegaard's most famous parable about worship is nicknamed "The Prompter," the person in the theater who helps the actors remember their lines if they go blank. He says that for most churchgoers we think of the ministers as the actors, the ones up on stage whom we have come to watch. We are in the seats, so like an audience in the theater, we are passive. Kierkegaard turned that around, suggesting that the ministers are prompters, helping the actors remember their lines and that the actors are none other than the congregation themselves. If there's an audience, he said, it would be God.[2]

Whether we be clergy or laity, this is quite the stretch for many of us, thinking of the congregation as the ones who act out the day's drama, the worship narrative unfolding. Think about it: most people coming to church on a given Sunday enter the building just moments before the "show" starts. If they were the players, they couldn't do that, right? They'd get there early. Someone hands them a program, I mean, an order of worship. They find their seats much like people do in the theater. And sure enough, the professionals do most of the work. If they like the performance, they might come back next week.

Kierkegaard's prompter parable focuses on one key dynamic in worship, maybe the most important of all, participation. Ideally, ministers serve as prompters who help the congregation become participants in the grand drama. Even though some people still think the word *liturgy* refers to some kind of pipe organ cathedral, it literally translates as, "the work of the people." When we worship, we're supposed to take part, not sit back. Rodney Clapp notes that if the writers of the New Testament had wanted worship to be private and for the congregations' entertainment, they could have chosen another word altogether, *orgia*, from which we get our word "orgy," not so much having to do with sexual debauchery but a self-absorbed excessive indulgence. They chose instead a word that means the "work of the people."[3]

Participation may well be the rarest commodity in our church's worship gatherings today. The architecture we have inherited and the patterns we have established promote passive audiences, not active participants, and that's true in both traditional and contemporary services in most places. We have lulled people into watching the show called worship.

Participation was one of the key aspects of the symposium, that after-dinner talk over wine that those first Christians practiced. The leader of the symposium made sure everyone could participate. You get a sense of the importance of involvement by all in Paul's words to the church at Corinth, "When you come together, each one has a hymn, a lesson, a revelation, a tongue, or an interpretation. Let all things be done for building up" (1 Cor 14:26). That's what a symposium was supposed to strive towards, everyone participating.

Unfortunately, that didn't always happen. Greco-Roman culture often promoted debates after dinner, different persons trying to prove their point of view as superior to others. In some ways, similar to how those first Christians strove for inclusion despite their privileged seating arrangements, they also strove for participation by all even if some voices were more arrogant than others. I suspect most of us have sat next to persons like that at a dinner party.

But in the first century if everyone might bring something to eat, they might also bring something to contribute to the potluck conversation. Much as the human body has different parts with different functions, Paul reminded those earliest followers of Jesus they had something to contribute to the body we now call church.

* * *

On any given Sunday nowadays churches meet to worship, services usually consisting of ten to twenty elements, things like: prelude, announcements, call to worship, prayer, offering, sermon, hymns, Communion, benediction, and postlude. Some traditions use other words for these elements, and some of them print bulletins, others not so much with the use of projectors and screens, but pretty much in every expression of worship around the world the service consists of ten to twenty elements. This is quite the contrast with those earliest Christian gatherings, with their twofold evening together: a supper and a symposium. Hard to imagine a bulletin with just those two words printed.

Some scholars refer to the symposium as a "drinking party" or "second tables." (I suspect the latter would be a better option for most congregations, since in my background a "drinking party" was rarely spiritual in nature.) Besides, "second tables" indicates a shift of sorts, from the meal to a time of entertainment and/or conversation. In the first century this shift involved some common rituals, although no one ever thought of one part of the evening as more sacred than another. They removed the central table on which the food had sat, swept the floor, and mixed wine with water in large bowls, three being the ideal number.

As my good friend and theologian Bill Stancil pointed out to me, at dinner parties in our homes these days it's common for hosts to suggest everyone move to the living room, not so much to signal a shift in tone but so that everyone might be comfortable and enter into a fuller conversation. That's a different kind of shift, seems to me.

In terms of the agenda at those first-century symposiums, there were several things that could take place before the conversation. A girl might play songs on a flute, apparently a favorite of many first-century diners. Or a young woman might dance like the daughter of Herodias did for Herod's birthday banquet in Mark 6. (There's nothing sexual or sinful implied in the Greek words of that story by the way. She danced, period. What was sinful was the request on her mother's part and her going along with it, the beheading of John the Baptist.)

In most worship services today music takes two expressions: that which we are invited to participate in (congregational singing) and that which we listen to (songs sung by choirs and ensembles, or instrumental music played). Obviously, congregational singing more naturally promotes participation, so it would be easy to dismiss the latter in an attempt to involve everyone, but not necessarily. Dinner church or otherwise, a lot of people have musical gifts that we should celebrate. In the spirit of Paul's letters to the churches, the goal would be promoting unity and participation by all in whatever form the music took.

There were also party games people might play at the symposium, one of the more popular called *kottabos*, the object being to fling the remaining droplets of wine from the rim of your glass into one of the large bowls in the center of the room, the winner receiving a cake or some sweet treat.[4] (I don't recommend that game if you meet in a place that has carpet and the wine is red.) The entertainment promoted festive joy among all. It's hard to imagine playing party games in a modern sanctuary, true, although I suspect many small groups and house churches have found games to be a wonderful time of bonding. The goal would be the opposite of the board game *Monopoly*, seeking instead to promote unity. (And I'm not just saying that because our son always wins. Always.)

The main part of the symposium, however, was a conversation, a time of talking that promoted participation by all. These conversations were the forerunner to what we now call sermons, which in our day are mostly monologues. This is something we need to discuss.

What We Talk about When We
Talk about Preaching

If you pay close attention to movie critics, even book critics, they often use the word *preaching* as the worst insult to hurl at a film or novel: "it preaches" or is "too preachy." Some people I know who do not write or read reviews of any kind don't care for the term either. They are allergic to *preaching*, not just the act itself, even the word. They break out in hives and run at the mere mention of it. If you count yourself among them, before you sprint off or close this book, look again at the name of this chapter, "The Conversation." Is that better?

In the interest of full disclosure—and I'm pretty sure I've made this clear in these pages already—I love preaching. I like the word. I like to preach. I like to read about preaching (even on the beach), think about preaching, help others think about preaching. It only figures since I'm a professor of preaching and worship. (Honestly, I can't believe the seminary pays me to think about and teach preaching. When I have to grade papers and serve on committees, then I recall how I earn a living. The rest of the time it's a gift.)

But I must confess some newly acquired resistance to the term on my part. I have developed some reservations about *preaching*. This is not the kind of opposition I've seen the last ten years or so in various churches, where instead of calling a sermon a "sermon," they opt instead for "teaching" or some such thing. That's a con game, near as I can tell, bait and switch. These "teachings" are deeper explorations of the text and/ or topic, but also longer. Much longer. I would like to run from those. Apparently, some folks want to sit still for forty-five minutes while the preacher dives into the intricacies of the text. Not me, and not because I don't love such digging. I do.

No, my real resistance isn't to the traditional language or the length or the depth of this preaching; it's about the lack of participation on the part of the congregation. I almost wrote, on the part of the "listeners," but even that term treats the congregation as silent partners, not as people with something to contribute.[5] In some traditions preachers will often pray a prayer just before the Scripture reading and sermon, what is sometimes referred to as a prayer of illumination. One of the most common is a line borrowed from Psalm 19:14, "May the words of my mouth and the meditations of all our hearts be acceptable unto you, O Lord, our rock and our redeemer." Maybe you've heard ministers who pray that line or you are a minister drawn to that prayer yourself. It is a nice thought. It wasn't until just recently, however, that I realized the stark contrast of roles in that prayer, namely those who get to have words in their mouths (the preachers) and those who only get to meditate in their hearts (the congregants). Jesus' disciples were always encouraged to raise their hands if they had a question, and they had lots of questions. Or to put it another way, Fred Craddock claims that in the traditional preaching set up, if the congregation is on the team, it is as javelin catcher.[6]

Rabbi Harold Kushner (best known for his book *When Bad Things Happen to Good People*) has more recently written about the changing landscape of religious traditions. He notes that when he was in rabbinical school he was taught, "These answers are the essence of Judaism. If your congregants ask you questions to which these answers don't fit, educate them to ask more appropriate questions." Sad to say, but Christians do something similar. Kushner writes, "In the twenty-first century, the religious agenda will be set not by tradition's answers but by congregants' questions."[7] I think he's right.

In light of the notion of participating in the sermon, there is another Greek word we should consider, *perichoresis*. (Normally you'd have to enroll in seminary and pay tuition to learn this much Greek vocabulary, so consider yourself lucky.) There are parts of this word you recognize, even if it doesn't seem likely. We get the word "choreography" from *choresis*; it refers to a dance. The preposition *peri* means around or about, as with a "perimeter." So literally *perichoresis* refers to a kind of dancing around or about. Most theologians aren't really interested in dancing, but they like this term and use it to designate the nature of God, in particular the three-in-one nature of God, or the Trinity.[8] The idea is that rather than imaging a hierarchy, the three are interdependent and interrelated, joining hands in a grand dance together. It's a lovely image for God. It's also a lovely image for human community. We are invited to live as God does, all of us joining hands in a grand dance.

Another way this image can be applied is in relation to preaching, although I'm not thinking about some flamboyant preachers who dare to dance while preaching. Heaven help us! No, applied to preaching we might think about the divine dance between three partners: preacher, people, and text. As you probably know, this relationship is typically more hierarchical in nature, with the preacher and text clearly standing over the congregation. What a convenient arrangement, huh, the preacher getting to be the Apostle Paul who once again chides those wayward Corinthians, or maybe Moses who scolds the children of Israel. Even Jesus correcting the disciples or those troublemaker Pharisees.

But this simply won't work, the preacher and text off somewhere dancing by themselves. The Scriptures do not belong to the preacher alone but the whole church, of which the minister is a part. Besides, at one moment of the dance the text might lead, asking questions of preacher and people; at another moment, however, the questions might flow the other direction, questioning the violence or misogyny in many passages. Preaching is supposed to be a dynamic dance.

When those first Christians inherited the pattern of a symposium after dinner, there were a variety of conversation patterns. Many banquets were philosophical in nature, with those present either voting on a topic of discussion for the evening or working through a fairly standard list of philosophical topics (truth, beauty, justice, etc. Some scholars think Paul's beautiful poem on love in 1 Corinthians 13 was just such a piece for a symposium[9]). Sometimes a professional speaker might be hired to talk on a subject. There were lots of variations in these gatherings because there were lots of different dining clubs.

It's easy to see how over time the conversation among Christians became less participatory, especially with the rise of professional clergy, morphing into the monologue sermons most of us are familiar with today. When was the last time you participated in a dialogical sermon? In many ways the preaching that takes place in our churches is like watching a chef prepare a meal but never getting to taste it. We just watch.

I obviously believe in an educated clergy, for the same reasons I believe in educated physicians and nurses. But an educated clergy doesn't mean the congregation doesn't have something to say as well. As Harvey Cox puts it, "Human beings might be defined as *Homo quaerens*, the stubborn creatures who cannot stop asking why and then asking why they ask why."[10]

In recent years there has been a growing emphasis on dialogue in preaching. Unfortunately, it has remained mostly a metaphor. For instance, one scholar writes about preaching using the image of gathering at a round table where sharing takes place. That seems promising, and it is, but not as promising as you might think. The idea, and it's a really good one, would be for the pastor to gather a select group of lay folks midweek to discuss the sermon from the previous week as well as the one upcoming. While the group is carefully chosen to represent the diversity of the congregation, even rotating people on and off of the roundtable gathering, an actual dialogue during church never takes place.[11] What a shame. As it turns out, lots of preaching scholars value dialogue in preaching *theory*, but not so much in *practice*.[12]

If dialogue is such a powerful metaphor, why must it remain metaphorical? Actually, I think I know why. Because opening up the sermon time for discussion is downright scary. Trust me, I speak from experience. A few semesters back I offered a preaching elective, Preaching with Postmoderns. Before we get bogged down in what postmodernism means, the preposition "with" is quite telling, implying a relationship between preacher and congregation, less of a top-down model in which preachers often preached "at" folks. (To be clear, even monological preaching can be "with" in its style, although the congregation's part of the conversation remains internal or symbolic at best.)

I had been reading about preaching and postmodernism for many years, but it was David Lose's little book, *Preaching at the Crossroads*, that made me draw a line in the sand.[13] Something needed to be done. (When theologians draw a line in the sand that usually means a new class offering. So that's what I did.) Contrary to popular opinion, postmodernism isn't necessarily a questioning of whether or not objective truth exists (according to postmoderns, such universal truths might exist, could very well exist), but more a suspicion about those who claim to have such easy access to those truths. In other words, how is it that a preacher can claim to know the answers? Sure, the minister went to seminary, but does that guarantee access to the mind of God? The topic is obviously more complicated than that, and Lose does an excellent job of addressing it, which is what we did in that class all semester.

Lose identifies three strategies for preaching in a postmodern context, but his emphasis on dialogue was a major focus of the class.[14] Whenever I bring up the term *dialogical preaching*, I can usually sense confusion on the other person's part, but of course that's the beauty of dialogue: we can talk together about the subject, about what I mean and what the congregation thinks about that. Turns out, there are a lot of dialogical options available to preachers. If you're a preacher or a congregant, try imagining these scenarios in your church, or perhaps in a dinner church meeting in a coffee shop. Rather than comment on each option, let me start with a simple listing of the possibilities, framed in one of three ways: before, during, and after the sermon. Be warned, some of them are quite scary.

Before the sermon could include discussions about the upcoming Sunday's sermon/conversation in a number of formats: meeting mid-week with an appointed but rotating group of lay leaders (as I already described); meeting midweek with anyone who wished to talk about this week's Scripture passage; posting questions and comments to social media ahead of Sunday where an online exchange might take place; and conversations in the daily rhythms of life and church.

During the sermon could include: discussion among parishioners, giving people a few minutes to discuss ideas being raised; open-ended questions addressed to the congregation, who are then encouraged to respond aloud; letting someone in the congregation share a story about the topic, pre-arranged or not; letting the congregation listen to a dialogue between two people (maybe the minister and someone else) who have thought about this together prior to the gathering; and encouraging questions and observations by the congregation via social media such as Twitter, with the tweets projected on a screen or selected by the minister. This last one using Twitter is being done in some places with mixed results.

After the sermon could include: a talk-back time of Q and A with the minister; a talk-back time when anyone can share their reflections, maybe tell another story brought to mind but without response on the minister's part; a midweek follow-up study on the previous sermon topic; social media postings during the week on the topic from last time; and the ongoing conversations of the group in daily life.

Does anyone else have high blood pressure about now? This scares the bejesus out of me, seriously. But as I told my students, it has the same dangers inherent in all relationships. Will there be someone who dominates, or tries to dominate the conversation? Someone else who makes no sense at all? Still another who is coherent but whose ideas are absurd? Yep! We all have family members who try such things at the Thanksgiving table, and it is the same with our Christian families when gathered at the table. It does help to remember every symposium needs a leader, someone to keep things on track. Those guidelines for first-century banqueting are so helpful. There will also be some amazing insights shared too.

If you want to get at least a glimpse of what can happen when the floor is open to more voices than just the preacher's, check out the classic book *The Gospel in Solentiname* by Ernesto Cardenal. Ministering among the peasants of Nicaragua during the Somoza dictatorship, Cardenal opted for dialogue in the place of traditional sermons. The community of peasants would read a Gospel passage together, then talk about it. The book is a people's commentary on the Gospels but also a glimpse into the power of communal sharing. Sure, sometimes it gets off track, but as Cardenal notes, "It was the Spirit who made them speak—the same Spirit who inspired the gospels."[15] Besides, when things got off track too far, he would offer some textual insights from his own scholarship to help guide them back. There's no reason for a dialogical sermon to result in chaos. Honestly, while dialogical preaching scares me, it also excites me.

A couple of winters ago I met with a group of pastors in the Kansas City area. They had received a grant to bring in guests like myself as they thought about different trends in ministry and such. They asked me to talk about preaching, and so among the different topics we discussed, dialogical preaching was one of them. I talked for a while to get the ball rolling, then opened the floor up for dialogue. Just as the first person was getting ready to say something, I interrupted, "Oh, never mind. I'll do all the talking today. You can just listen, meditate in your hearts if you like." We all laughed.

* * *

On three separate occasions the semester I taught that elective on postmodernism, I joined my students in the experiment, preaching a dialogical sermon. Because I'm an introvert, and probably for other psychological reasons beyond my recognition, I chose post-sermon dialogue. We sang a hymn after the sermon, and then opened up the floor for a time of response. I even sat in such a place so as not to focus attention on me, but rather let their collective voices occupy the center of attention.

Nothing. No one said a word, and for a long time. Thirty seconds of silence is a long time in our churches. This felt like thirty minutes of no one saying a word. Why would they? I mean the first liturgical lesson of childhood came from a parent shushing us. We can't expect participation without preparing the congregation. But I didn't budge, didn't let it show that I was hoping someone would at least say something. Then a trickle turned to a lively time of conversation among us all. It is hard to describe just how fun this was, listening to people tell stories and make comments. I suppose what might capture it is *euphrosyne*, "festive joy." I've lost count of how many times after worship I've had someone share something with me that I wish everyone in the congregation could have heard. I can't help but think that in the years to come more and more sermons will be dialogical in one way or another. People will not only bring covered dishes to a dinner church gathering, but some thoughts about the Bible passage under consideration as well, thoughts they actually get to share.

The ironic thing about this one sermon I repeated and the ensuing time of dialogue is that it was on the church's early eucharistic practices. It didn't occur to me then, but while I was preaching on the joyful supper of our ancestors in the faith, we were all participating in a symposium. Minus the part about flinging wine into bowls.

Talking at the Table

After I had my eucharistic epiphany in Arkansas back in 1999 and my ordination recognized in the Christian Church (Disciples of Christ), I naturally got more invitations to preach in churches whose practice was weekly Eucharist. In my days as a Baptist minister, Communion could be as infrequently as once a month, and if you happened to miss that Sunday, well, too bad. Now I was preaching every week with the table in full view. It had always been in full view of course, but instead of a large Bible and some chrysanthemums on it, there was now bread and wine. We had gathered to *eat* at this table.

It is hard for me to describe the difference between a sermon that will be followed by Communion and one that will not. Some of my minister friends in traditions that don't celebrate at the table every week claim it's not hard to tell the difference at all. A couple of my Presbyterian minister friends joked that the sermons are simply shorter on Communion Sunday, sometimes even labeled differently, "homily" or "meditation," to signal the brevity.

Actually I have never really felt the constraints of time because the Disciples congregations I know are so efficient at serving Communion that it only takes a few minutes anyway. You should see our denominational gathering when we serve thousands of people in just a few minutes. I wonder if there's a category in the *Guinness Book of World Records* for such things? Let's hope not.

For me, the difference isn't time and not necessarily theme. Yes, my sermons have often focused on eucharistic imagery when appropriate, but not every week. For me the difference is a matter of feel. I honestly don't know if I can explain this, and apparently I'm not alone either because I've noticed over the years that when my peers write professional papers about this topic—what it means to preach at the table or what we might designate a eucharistic homiletic—they're not very good at describing the difference either. The one exception is Charles Rice in his book, *The Embodied Word*, a volume that influenced me in ways I didn't even realize when I first read it more than twenty years ago.[16]

But there is something different about preaching when it happens at a table. It even sounds odd to think about preaching at a table, depending of course on what you think preaching is or should be. I will never forget one sermon I preached at a table. A minister friend who shall remain nameless had invited me to preach a stewardship sermon at his church, a Sunday in November, the final one in a fall campaign as they thought about the budget and ministries of the church for the next year. The usual sort of thing, right? Well, not exactly. Oh, sure, that Sunday was normal, but the beginning of that stewardship season was anything but normal.

My friend said that not only did he want me to preach on that final Sunday, but to help the stewardship team think about the campaign as it was getting underway. There would be a banquet prior to the campaign, with the eight or so team members there, and their significant others if they chose. It was scheduled for a weeknight in a nearby Italian restaurant. I kept picturing a banquet room, doors closed, and a measure of privacy. Sure, there would be wait staff there, but near the end of the evening they would give us some privacy and I would preach. Even for an introvert, this seemed doable.

Only it turns out, we were not in a banquet room, but in the restaurant itself. Not the proverbial "smack dab" middle, but close enough. For the life of me, I could not imagine standing up in that place and preaching. All through the meal I felt panicked. Picture this: waiters and waitresses delivering plates of cheesecake, filling water glasses, people at nearby tables enjoying their spaghetti, and suddenly a stranger at the table near them stands up with a Bible in his hand. Did I mention a tune by Frank Sinatra was playing over the speakers? How does one preach about the way of the Lord when Old Blue Eyes is singing about doing it his way? How does one preach at a table? I mumbled my way through, but it was not pretty.

Obviously that is not what we mean by preaching at the table in the life of the church. But preaching at the so-called Lord's table is different, and I do mean *at* the table. For several years I was a member of Saint Andrew Christian Church in the Kansas City area, one of the most amazing churches I have ever been part of. The first time I preached there, I realized two things right away: 1) there is no pulpit and thus, no place for a preacher to have notes; and 2) without a pulpit, the preachers in that church stand at the table, a lovely round one pretty much in the center of their space.

Even on the Sundays when the sermon had nothing to say about the meal we would be eating, I and all the other ministers who served there stood at the table. I think one of the ways such preaching is different is how I began to realize the sermon didn't have to be the central act, the main attraction. There was an opening song each week that reminded us we had gathered to eat while someone held the bread and cup before us, and there was the climactic moment each week, eating that meal together. The sermon, in some ways, got us ready for that, assuming the meal comes afterwards and not before as it did for those earliest followers of Jesus.

I think the other way preaching at the table differs from the traditional delivery from the pulpit is the tone that is set by talking over a meal. A conversational style seems more fitting when gathered at the table. Fred Craddock, who revolutionized preaching theory in the 1970s, discovered this as well. One of the men in his church asked him why he was so much more interesting when gathered in the fellowship hall telling stories over plates of pie than when preaching in the sanctuary. While that must have hurt at the time, thank God for that man's question. As a result, Craddock introduced a more narrative and conversational style of preaching to the sanctuary.

One of the things I loved about Dinner Church in Brooklyn was how the minister, a guest preacher the Sunday I was there, stood up while the people were still eating (although maybe seated might be a better posture). In fact, folks are encouraged to keep on eating. I did something similar when I preached at that college and career gathering headed up by Joy and Elliott. Rather than wait for everyone to finish eating, which is rather typical at banquets and such these days, I got up roughly midway through their supper. I encouraged them to keep eating as I read the Bible passage. I made observations about the text, told stories, the usual things preachers do. But I also encouraged conversation at each table and then among us all, the whole time maintaining a more conversational style myself.

The goal of this approach to preaching isn't to sneak up on people with the gospel while they're enjoying a chocolate chip cookie, as if food will make them more susceptible to what a preacher has to say. No, the goal is participation, give-and-take, even if some introverts within the congregation might choose not to talk.

One of the objections often raised to dialogical preaching has to do with authority, the authority of the pulpit and the clergy itself. During the Protestant Reformation of the sixteenth century, this was a major point of emphasis. In my Preaching with Postmoderns class, even the more laid back of my students admitted reluctance to let go of their authority. They were earning Masters degrees, after all. Did that count for nothing?

I get that, but I'm not convinced all the authority preachers have claimed is necessary, nor am I convinced that preachers can't retain some appropriate level of expertise (perhaps a better term than authority) in a conversational setting. For starters, even in Paul's day while house churches promoted conversations after dinner, he still names gifts of apostles, prophets, and teachers, indicating different levels of responsibility during such conversations.[17] This is likely what happened in that story in Acts 20, when poor Eutychus fell out the window; Paul wasn't droning on all by himself. The text says that after the boy was resurrected, Paul "continued to converse with them" (Acts 20:11). Note the preposition.

I love the analogy Wes Allen offers in his book *The Homiletic of All Believers*, the preacher's sermon like the sharing of a photo album, the conversation about the various images there. Anyone can make comments about a particular photo, clergy or laity. But the preacher brings a trained eye. The preacher is the one who has decided on what picture to share and who gets the conversation started. "Through their homiletical cameras, they artistically offer new perspectives of what the congregation has been looking at all along," whether in the biblical text or daily life. And of course the congregation may well see things the preacher has missed.[18] The goal is participation, even if the preacher is the one bringing the sermon, or maybe more accurately, the beginnings of a sermon. Everyone is encouraged to contribute.

Rethinking Worship

If this were a class in seminary, surely we would have had a test by now, a pop quiz at least, or as we near the end, a final exam. There would be essay questions for sure but vocabulary as well. After all, we've covered so many terms that would need to be defined and discussed, important Greek words for sure: *deipnon* (supper), *symposion* (conversation after dinner), *euphrosyne* (festive joy), and *parousia* (coming, as in Christ's coming again), to name a few. There is one word, however, we have not talked about directly, even though we have talked around it all along: worship. In the spirit of those first-century symposiums, this is a topic for conversation we desperately need to have, and preferably over a meal. But while that's not possible here in these pages, it might be just the thing for you and some friends to do.

Honesty, when I began this book I didn't see this topic coming, not directly. I wanted us to rethink how we eat Communion; I had no idea it would mean rethinking worship too. Like a lot of denominations, the United Methodists have different slogans from time to time. As I write, theirs is "Rethink Church," a slogan meant to suggest this is a new day for doing church. In that spirit, I invite us to rethink worship as well. You might think the omission of a discussion on "worship" up to this point is obvious, because, well, everyone already knows what it means. Some people go to church most every Sunday, and some never go, but even among the latter camp, most everyone has experienced (or survived) worship services at some point. There might be many styles available these days—traditional, contemporary, and a blending of those two—three flavors, so to speak, compared to the proverbial thirty-one flavors of ice cream offered at Baskin Robbins, but worship is worship. You know, worship.

Turns out, this may well be the hardest term to define because in part it has many meanings. As Andrew McGowan notes, the word can be used nowadays to describe a communal gathering (like what happens in many churches on Sundays), an inward devotion (the basis for those outward expressions when gathered or alone), even a particular genre of music in some places (also called praise songs). As he goes on to note, when the seventeenth-century translators of the King James Version chose the word *worship* (from the Old English "worth-ship," as in ascribing worth) for different Hebrew terms in the Old Testament and Greek words in the New Testament, they pretty much restricted themselves to acts of obedience and service toward God, not Sunday gatherings like we're used to. (That's still true with modern translations as well.)

In his provocatively titled book, *God Against Religion*, Matthew Myer Boulton suggests that the very idea of worshiping God was not the original divine plan for us. Drawing on the story of Adam and Eve in the garden, he shows how humans were meant to be intimate friends with God in that paradise, not worshipers. Boulton writes, "There is no temple in paradise, and in that sense, no liturgy." The so-called *work of the people*, which you will recall is what the word *liturgy* means, does not exist in the garden of Eden. Whatever work is to be done there is done with God, not alone or separate from God.

Then the serpent enters, with his questions about God. Note the preposition. Intimacy *with* God turns into questions *about* God, "Did God say, 'You shall not eat from any tree in the garden?'" As Boulton notes, "If God is at hand, then obviously the question is better put to God." But living "east of Eden"—the language Genesis uses to describe life outside of paradise—worship becomes one way among many that humans will relate to God, perhaps even seek to earn God's pleasure. Boulton shows how that encounter in the garden, the one between the first couple and the serpent, was the world's first worship service so to speak, complete with sermon and supper. After misinterpreting God's commands about the fruit and after eating from the one tree prohibited, their eyes are opened to their nakedness. It's not that worship is somehow sinful, but it turns out to be a wonderful occasion for sin, especially human pride.

Something similar happens among their offspring, the boys Cain and Abel, their worship offerings leading to murder (Gen 4). Boulton summarizes when he says that "the story of humanity's fall and of liturgy's rise is the same story . . . . East of Eden, people disguise and develop their work into full-blown worship, and the personal disorientation of the garden ('Where are you?') is matched by the social disorientation of the field ('Where is your brother?')." The larger story of Adam and Eve, along with their offspring, ends with this telling verse: "At that time, people began to invoke the name of the Lord" (Gen 4:26).[19] The invention of worship. At roughly the same time these stories in Genesis were being written down, prophets like Micah and Amos were claiming God hated their religious festivals, preferring instead justice for the poor and marginalized.[20]

This notion of our inventing worship is consistent with the New Testament as well, where the word *worship* refers to how we live our lives, as Paul does for example in Romans 12:1, describing the presenting of our bodies as a living sacrifice as "spiritual worship." Communal gatherings would have simply been one way among many for expressing this devotion to God.

There's just no simple way to look at the Bible for a definition of what we now think of as worship services. McGowan concludes, "While then as now there was communal eating and drinking, music, symbol, prayer, Scripture, teaching, and those other things that now constitute 'worship' as variously understood, we must admit something difficult at the outset: in the ancient world, what we now call 'worship' did not quite exist."[21] Let that last phrase sink in.

Robert Banks reaches a similar conclusion when he notes that Paul's failure to say anything about a person going to church *to worship* is "one of the most puzzling features of Paul's understanding" of church altogether. Worship is how life was lived, whereas first-century gatherings (a much more accurate term) were all about the community of people there.[22] In the sermon we call Hebrews (typically thought of as one of the New Testament's *epistles*), there is a verse about "not neglecting to meet together, as is the habit of some," except the point isn't *worshiping God*. Instead the verse continues, "but encouraging one another" (Heb 10:25). Another emphasis on the "one another" aspect of those earliest gatherings.

One of the many reasons we don't have a description or definition of worship services in the Bible is because all those Christ followers already knew what they were doing when they gathered. They didn't need to be told, and certainly couldn't imagine they would need to tell us. Instead, what we get in the New Testament are glimpses, or maybe better yet, little pieces of the jigsaw puzzle, but definitely not the big picture on the cover of the box. Those "pieces" are contained in the various epistles of Paul and others, since as the theory goes, these letters would have been read aloud during the symposium part of their gatherings. For instance, some have suggested that the opening salutations of those epistles might have been the way they greeted one another when gathered for their dinner parties, "Grace to you and peace from God our Father and the Lord Jesus Christ" (Rom 1:7), although such formalities could have developed later. Or endings such as, "The grace of the Lord Jesus be with you" as a way to bless each other as they departed (1 Cor 16:23). There are even fragments of hymns in some of those epistles that could have been sung at their communal times when gathered (Col 1:15–20 and Phil 2:6–11) even if they don't always appear musically formatted in our Bibles.[23] What we don't know is how any of those things might have flowed the way we normally think of an order of worship.

But the larger issue here is that what we now call a *worship service* didn't really take place; it was more of a social gathering, and since that was part of their lives, it would qualify as one of the ways a person's life is *worship*. The idea that worship as we know it didn't really exist has taken me by surprise, and perhaps even now it is upsetting your own equilibrium. I get that, I do. When I introduced this notion to my students, it caused quite a buzz on campus. This distinction between those early dinner parties and our church services has everything to do with our orientation. Let me explain.

In my Intro to Worship course I have always stressed the importance of a theocentric focus in our modern worship services, the focus on God. We sing songs to God, we offer our praises to God, we pray to God. This is what we typically do on any given Sunday. Worship is aimed toward God. Sure, God also speaks to us (in sermons, in quiet times, and other ways); and yes, we speak to each other in worship (greeting one another, praying for each other, we even sing some songs to each other, "Sister, let me be your servant," for example) but the main focus is Godward, primarily vertical. This counteracts our cultural tendency to be self-absorbed, to be entertained. As I sometimes tell my students, worship is not about how many goose bumps we experience but about offering ourselves to God.

As much as I believe in such an orientation (although I do have my doubts), that simply wasn't the case in those earliest decades when believers gathered. Their Eucharistic banquets weren't self-centered, true, but neither were they primarily God-centered; it was more community-centered. In a phrase, more about fellowship than worship.

This emphasis on community rather than what we normally think of as worship was true from the very beginning, even when the Christ followers were still part of Judaism, meeting in synagogues as well as house churches because contrary to popular opinion, synagogues weren't initially so much places of worship as cultural centers and educational spaces.[24] As my rabbi friend Michael Zedek recently confirmed, synagogues were more about study and fellowship, but even those things were (and still are) considered "worship" in Jewish thought, the way one's whole life is lived. Even the seating arrangement in synagogues was less like the theater, which can promote a passive audience.

For centuries the Temple was the place of worship for Jews, offering sacrifices to God, until the Romans destroyed it in the year 70. After that, for the Jews their worship would take place in the synagogue much as it does today. For those early Christians, house churches constituted their "synagogue" so to speak (the word means "gathering place"). But the point is these gatherings were more fellowship than anything we might call worship, for Jews as well as Christians.

As I noted earlier, those first-century ancestors of ours didn't have dinner together (*deipnon*), fellowshipping and such, only to reorient themselves toward God as they moved into the second part of the evening (*symposion*). "Okay, if you'll finish your meal, we're moving into a time of worship. Leave your wine glasses here." No, nothing like that. The whole evening was oriented toward enjoying each other's company, building each other up, promoting unity. All of this, as with all of life, was done in the presence of God. Obviously things have changed. This kind of community orientation is now common among small groups, but not so much in our larger worship gatherings.

Diana Butler Bass describes the traditional way of doing worship as "vertical theology," the church serving as a kind of elevator, taking people up into the presence of God who sits in the heavens. (Matthew Fox cleverly labels it "worshup.")[25] Bass notes that cultural shifts seem to be leading toward a more horizontal way of thinking, with a stress on God's presence among us, even in creation.[26] Here's one way to think about the difference between vertical worship as we know it and those early horizontal gatherings. Typically, on a given Sunday we orient ourselves toward God while gathered in the presence of others, whereas in a horizontal gathering such as a dinner church the idea is to orient ourselves toward our brothers and sisters in Christ while in the presence of God. You might want to reread that last sentence.

True, by the middle of the second century Christians began to develop a more organized and more vertical form of gathering, at least in some places, and since the fourth century until now, vertical, not horizontal, has been the primary way we orient ourselves when gathered on Sundays in the sanctuary. But this is something we developed, not necessarily something God intended. Christianity has developed all sorts of practices through the centuries (a season of Lent, walking a prayer labyrinth, etc.) as well as doctrines (worship is primarily for God, God is three persons and yet one, here's what happens when we eat this meal, etc.). I have loved many of these things, and some of them I still do, including the tradition of robed ministers with gorgeous stoles around their necks. But all of these things are developments, and I'm having difficulty imagining me in my ministerial robe at a dinner party.

In the late nineteenth century the theologian John Henry Newman compared such doctrinal developments to the way a river's course changes over time. But of course these developments can be reconsidered because not every change is good. If the math is right, that Christianity holds a giant garage sale every five hundred years, getting rid of some things that we once cherished, now seems to be a ripe time for reconsidering these churchly developments. Some would call this thinking outside the box, but in truth, the vertical worship services that developed over time are outside of the box those earliest followers knew.

Of the four characteristics of those earliest Christian dinner parties, vertical worship has led to a diminishment of two of them for sure: intimacy and involvement. Worshiping God in the presence of others has meant that in many ways we hardly know the people around us. It's more like the symphony than church; the people next to us just happen to have tickets like we do and we just happen to be sitting on the same row. Horizontal church reminds us that we are brothers and sisters, gathered to fellowship with and encourage one another. Ministers in vertical worship often try to remind people of this, but that's easier to do in horizontal gatherings because it's the main focus.

But if horizontal gatherings are great at connecting us with others, we will have to work harder at reminding ourselves we are gathered in the presence of God. Instead of challenging worshipers to grow closer to God, a fairly common plea in vertical church, we will need to help each other recognize that we are always in God's presence, but that we just aren't always attuned to that fact. In his book *Flourishing*, theologian Miroslav Volf rightly claims that "attachment to God amplifies and deepens enjoyment of the world." He reminds us the world is God's gift to us. "Little trinkets on the shelves of gift stores are not gifts; they *become* gifts when somebody gives them to somebody else."[27] And that is what God has done with this world we live in. People in horizontal gatherings surround themselves with reminders of these gifts, most notably the food before us on the table, bread and wine, but also cheese and crackers.

Another challenge with vertical worship is how often it diminishes meaningful participation by those gathered. If Kierkegaard's "prompter" parable is right, then vertical worship encourages participation in a limited manner. For instance, it's common in many vertical services to include responsive readings. Some worship leader, clergy or layperson, reads the first line and the congregation reads the bold print or italics. Here's one that often signals a move toward Communion:

The Lord be with you.

And also with you.

Lift up your hearts.

We lift them up to the Lord.

There's a measure of participation when reading something like this, true, but must everyone say the same thing? What if some of us can't lift up our hearts right now? Some theologians have argued that what a responsive reading like this does is speak on behalf of those who are not in the same place as others. That's true enough, but what if I don't even want to be on the same page? What if my views are different from yours? Or in the case of a creed, what if some among us believe differently? The conversation of a symposium allowed for differing points of view.

Don't get me wrong; I still love going to vertical church on Sundays, especially Country Club Christian Church where I now serve on staff. Maybe you could say I have a lover's quarrel with the church. The Canadian theologian Douglas John Hall reminds us that the church is the bride of Christ, but the bride definitely has issues.[28] That's something of how I feel, but still I go, and not just because I'm not on staff at a church. Despite my so-so voice, I like congregational singing. And I like listening to sermons, good ones anyway. I like listening to a grand choir, or a beautiful piece on the piano or guitar. I love visiting with friends. I love church. Sad to say though, it's getting harder for me to attend typical Sunday services ever since I read about those first-century dinner parties and attended various models of dinner church.

I find myself drawn more and more to horizontal gatherings rather than vertical worship. To return to Diana Butler Bass's image, instead of thinking of the church as elevator, maybe a table would be more helpful. Rather than bemoan "the sky is falling" when it comes to the state of Christianity, we could be encouraged that focusing on the horizon may actually bring us closer to God, and to one another.

In their book *Church Refugees*, sociologists Josh Packard and Ashleigh Hope interviewed people who reluctantly and painfully had decided to leave church life altogether. They conclude, "Perhaps more than anything else, what people want out of a church is a community of people who are experiencing God together," with an emphasis more on the "together" part since one of the main reasons they fled in the first place was the church's stifling "people's ability to engage with each other and their communities."[29] Nancy Ammerman, who also studies religion from a sociological perspective, finds that the people with "the most robust sense of sacred presence in everyday life are those who participate in religious activities that allow for conversation and relationship."[30] I think she's right.

My hunch is that while horizontal movements are taking shape and catching on in many places, surely most churches will continue to have vertical worship services as well as smaller horizontal clusters throughout the week. No one can say for sure what is going to evolve. One thing is certain, this shift from vertical to more horizontal is something our churches will need to rethink in whatever future we shape together.

RSVP

"Look! I stand at the door and knock. If you hear my
voice and open the door, I will come in, and we will
share a meal together as friends."

—REVELATION 3:20 (NLT)

The Road to Emmaus

Long before online Evites came along, people hosting banquets issued
invitations. They could be written or delivered orally by servants, but
invitations constituted part of the social protocol, an obvious way to know
who was coming and who wasn't.[1] This was true for every banqueting club
in the first century, including the ones we now call church. I don't know
if first-century hosts faced the same challenges brides do these days with
wedding planning, allowing for a certain percentage to show or not, trying
to have enough food and drinks for everyone, but there is another aspect
of invitations often overlooked. Namely, the simple fact someone wants
another someone to be present.

I titled the first part of this book "An Invitation," and now I have
named the final part "RSVP," even if that's French and not Greek. Specifically, I'd like to extend three invitations to you the reader: past, present, and
future. The first invitation entails a look back at one more ancient biblical
story (The Road to Emmaus); the second offers a series of snapshots from
the dinner church movement presently unfolding (Living in Emmaus); and
the third invites us to explore and imagine what the church is becoming
and might someday be (The Future of Emmaus).

We start, then, with one more meal story in the New Testament, about
what happens when we gather as followers of the Christ. It was all I could

do to wait until now to bring it up because it's a favorite passage for many people, myself included, the poster child of eucharistic stories. It's an Easter story, only not just any Easter, but something that happened on the evening of that very first Easter just outside of Jerusalem. Here's how this particular story from Luke 24 unfolds: two travelers walk the road back home from Jerusalem to Emmaus, confounded and confused by all that has happened. What they do know for fact is that Jesus, the one from Nazareth whom they had loved and followed, is now dead. He was not just a friend; he embodied hope itself, the one who was going to run the Romans out of town, turn Israel's fortunes around. Not now. Their slumped shoulders tell it all, as they shuffle their sandaled feet along the dusty road, kicking rocks along the way. It was a seven-mile journey, but it might as well have been seven million miles. Jesus is dead, that much they know, and well, the fact that dead people don't come back to life.

That's when Jesus joins them, his resurrected feet kicking the same rocks as the travelers. Only they don't know it's him. You have to love the irony. Their eyes are "kept from recognizing" him, is how Luke tells it (Luke 24:16). What follows next is the first-century version of those TV shows that pull practical jokes on people. You've seen the type. Jesus is the show's host, which will be true in more ways than one. He asks them, "What are you talking about?" Cleopas, that's the name of one of them, responds, "What, are you kidding? Are you the only one around these parts that doesn't know what has happened?" That's when I picture Jesus winking at the hidden camera as he says, "What do you mean?" And the two of them stand still, heartbroken.

Cleopas and his companion begin to rehearse the story of all that Jesus did when he was alive. Only they rehearse this to Jesus himself. Jesus winks at the camera again as he softly chides them, "Are you so foolish as to have forgotten what Jesus said, about how he would be killed and rise again?" You have to appreciate the irony of a Bible story in which Jesus speaks of himself in third person. As Luke puts it, Jesus begins to preach a little sermon, a conversation really, from the Old Testament about the expected Messiah.

And the sermon does not get through to them, even a dialogical one. How's that for a plot twist? Even the preaching of the resurrected Jesus does not register. They finally arrive at the village of Emmaus, where Jesus pretends he is going to continue on down the road. But the couple invite him into their home, good first-century hospitality at work. "It's late. Stay with us."

"No, I really need to keep going. Well, okay, just for a minute, I guess." Wink, wink. So Jesus goes inside, where in keeping with such hospitality, they offer him bread. Suddenly Jesus becomes host at their table. He is the one who takes the bread and offers a blessing. In fact, he not only takes it and blesses it; he also breaks it and gives it to them, a familiar series of verbs.

The next thing you know, Jesus feeds them, and suddenly their eyes are opened, which would be a good ending, only that's not the end of the story. Instead of the two travelers "living happily ever after," Jesus vanishes. Completely disappears. *Candid Camera* gives way to a David Copperfield special, a magic show minus the lovely assistant. Suddenly the stage is empty, except for these two weary and dazed pilgrims. Cleopas and his companion are practically speechless, scratching their heads. Eyes now wide open, they look at each other. "Were not our hearts burning when he walked with us on the road, explaining the Scriptures?" Except if their hearts had been burning, there were no signs of it then.

Now the two of them run on the road where earlier they had shuffled, to Jerusalem they jog. Meanwhile, back in the Holy City the followers of Jesus are a mixed lot. The women who had been to the tomb have started to believe in the resurrection, but the men folk are slow to catch on, calling the women's testimony an "idle tale," although the Greek expression is closer to "a load of crap" (Luke 24:11). Eventually they take Simon Peter's word for it. When Cleopas and his companion get there, he tells how Jesus has appeared to them as well, in the breaking of bread.

But even that's not the end of the story. Jesus shows up again. He speaks words of peace, which his followers have been doing ever since, assures them there's no reason to be afraid, and asks a question that seems hard to believe, or maybe not if we have been reading our way through the whole of Luke's gospel, not little bits and pieces here and there. Jesus asks, "Do you have anything around here to eat?" Isn't that something? The one who has been raised from the dead and who will be recognized in the breaking of bread eats with them again. But even that's not the end of the story, because he will show up every Sunday after that and eat with whoever gathers together. Even us.

If they gave out Academy Awards for best Bible story, or more specifically "best short feature in a canonical Gospel," surely the road to Emmaus story would take home the little gold statue. It has so many twists and turns, so many features for such a short journey. For instance, there's a wonderful pattern to the whole last chapter of Luke's gospel, a kind of echo pattern (what scholars call a *chiasm*, from the Greek of course), starting with Scriptures and food—Jesus preaches to them before they eat (Luke 24:25–27, 30–31)—and then reversing that order with food and Scriptures—eating with all the disciples and then opening their minds to understand the Scriptures as the Third Gospel comes to a close (Luke 24:41–45).[2]

What if the story of that first "worship service" in the garden of Eden has been reversed here in Luke's gospel? Instead of a couple listening to the voice of the serpent where eating leads to eyes open to their sin, a couple listen to Jesus and eat with eyes open to the very presence of God's chosen one among them, at their very table. I wonder if this isn't Luke's way of reversing the garden of Eden story.

Or how about the fact archaeologists claim that the little village of Emmaus is one of those rare ancient sites never located. Luke says it was seven miles from Jerusalem, but evidently that is just not enough of a hint. There are literally no findings to indicate it ever existed. Frederick Buechner suggests maybe that's as it should be, so that Emmaus becomes code for the town where each of us goes about our business and where the Christ keeps showing up.[3]

Living in Emmaus

On the hit TV series *Shark Tank*, entrepreneurs with big dreams pitch ideas to five venture capitalists. If you've never seen an episode, it's quite entertaining. Some of the ideas are goofy, others brilliant, but it's the interactions with the sharks, the potential backers, that makes the formula work. I have no intentions of going on the show, although I do have an idea that is goofy and brilliant at the same time.

Most everyone is familiar with a chronograph, a fancy name for a wristwatch that sometimes features a built-in stopwatch, but is always associated with precision timekeeping. My device would be a kairograph. Like the word *chronograph*, my *kairograph* comes from the Greek. No surprise there.

In the Greek New Testament there are two terms for "time," *chronos* and *kairos*. The first has to do with the ticking of the clock, time as we usually think of it. The second isn't so much about ordinary time but a special time, quality rather than quantity. *Kairos* is used for example when Jesus begins his ministry announcing, "The time is fulfilled, and the kingdom of God has come near; repent, and believe in the good news" (Mark 1:15). *Kairos* entails a different way of telling time, a season of God's moving in a unique way.

So while your chronograph might tell you it's a few minutes after 11:00 in the morning, a kairograph would tell you that something different is going on, a movement of God, in this case a movement of dinner churches or horizontal gatherings, which near as I can tell found new life around 2008. The best-known one is St. Lydia's in Brooklyn, which I mentioned earlier, but there are lots of these communities being born. No question, many of God's churches are living in Emmaus today, gathering around tables. Verlon Fosner of Community Dinners in Seattle estimates a new dinner church is being planted about every three weeks, at least among the ones he knows, including in South Korea and Scotland. More about his vision for dinner church in a bit.

In these pages I thought I might share some of the models I've encountered in my own research and travels, a kind of album with snapshots from various dinner churches that have sprung up and are still springing up. Other than St. Lydia's in Brooklyn, there are so many amazing stories still unfolding, and I've been fortunate to visit some of these and to visit by phone with others. What follows isn't exhaustive by any means, but at least it features some snapshots.

* * *

Previously, I briefly mentioned The Open Table in Kansas City, curated by Nick Pickrell and Wendie Brockhaus. That's the language they use, curator. A few months after meeting Nick for coffee, my wife and I checked out a gathering of The Open Table. That's the word I would use, *gathering*. Because it's hosted in the church building at Second Presbyterian, their dinner is in the fellowship hall area, on the second and fourth Sunday evenings each month. During the warmer months of summer, they sit outdoors as the setting sun gives way to stars. The night we went the tables were arranged in a U shape, and with chairs on both sides of the table, the room aglow with candles. You could be inside or outside of the "u," but the idea was that there would be no outsiders. The folks at The Open Table take those words seriously, because at the table are not just the usual suspects but many who are living on the margins, eking out a living.

The meal was potluck, everything from enchiladas and salads (my wife made an amazing one with spinach and candied walnuts, with little pieces of bacon, even some blueberries too) to chips and brownies. While I enjoyed the feast, some of those persons on the margin went back for seconds, even thirds. Eating is different depending on one's social location, no question. So was the discussion time.

The speaker that night was one of my former students at the seminary, a woman named Laurie who spoke on immigration reform. I think the idea was for us to discuss the topic during dinner, but while there was a sheet of paper at every place setting to help get the conversation started, well, conversations are often potluck too. A woman near us with obvious mental challenges proved to be a different sort of conversation partner.

After dinner, we were invited to move into the church's parlor for music and a more focused conversation, something those earliest followers of Jesus would have recognized even if we had chairs for sitting rather than couches for reclining. At The Open Table they are so intentional about letting everyone know they're welcome to move into the parlor or welcome to stay around the tables and talk. The staff even designates a "lingerer" each week, someone to linger around the tables and make people feel comfortable whatever they choose to do.

Once in the parlor, Nick and some other musicians sang a couple of songs, the lyrics printed on a handout, although it didn't seem like any of us sitting there were expected to join in. It was great music though, and after that Laurie told us stories about the pain of deportation, how it splits up undocumented families. At several points she paused, inviting us to offer up images. She said, "What are some of the fears associated with people from other lands? What words do we hear tossed about, words that hurt?" Later she asked for words to describe our hopes for unity.

When she was through, we sang a final song and then Laurie closed us with a unison reading of the "Immigrant Apostles' Creed," that begins, "I believe in Almighty God, who guided the people in exile and in exodus, the God of Joseph in Egypt and Daniel in Babylon, the God of foreigners and immigrants. I believe in Jesus Christ, a displaced Galilean who was born away from his people and his home . . . ." It concludes, "I believe in life eternal, in which no one will be foreigner but all will be citizens of the kingdom where God reigns forever and ever. Amen." It was a powerful evening, to say the least, and in many ways because of the guest list. We were encouraged to remember those on the edge, some of whom were eating with us.

* * *

Verlon Fosner is a minister in the Assemblies of God tradition who not only oversees a dinner church ministry, but trains others interested in planting such a ministry themselves. That alone sets him apart. As far as I know, he's the only one to provide a manual as well, with attention to details like recipes. You can order all sorts of resources online through their website. If St. Lydia's in Brooklyn functions as ground zero for the progressive dinner church movement, Verlon's ministry serves a similar role for many evangelicals.

Sixteen years ago he started serving at Westminster Community Church in Seattle, which is so far from the Bible belt it's not even funny. The church was doing okay, but nothing great. So he and his wife dreamed up a lot of different ideas, the first five of which failed miserably, a fact he even posts on their website. But the sixth version was the charm, so to speak, a dinner church model based on the agape feasts of the second century, at least as near as they could tell.

They started over in 2009. Spread throughout various urban neighborhoods of Seattle, they now have five meeting places, one each on Monday through Thursday evenings and one on Sunday as well. The meetings are called Community Dinners, because that's what they are, dinners that happen in particular communities throughout the city. The smallest runs 100 in attendance, the largest nearly 300. That also sets them apart since most dinner churches typically try to stay small. In their case the intimacy happens not on a corporate level, but at each individual table around the room.

Food is served, and then folks sit at round tables with eight or so at each. The people around those tables are as diverse as the population, many of them living on the margins, not really churchgoing folks. Verlon describes the usual crowd as one-third "financially challenged," one-third "suffering from isolation," and one-third "good Samaritans that have shown up to help." While people are eating someone plays music and sings, not so much a time of congregational singing, although it often unfolds that way. People will push their plates back, turn toward the musician, and receive the musical offering as worshipful. They also have artists paint scenes inspired by different Gospel stories.

About midway through the ninety-minute gathering the lead pastor (there are five under him, one for each of the communities) tells a story about Jesus without much elaboration. They don't even think of it as a sermon per se. After that, there's a brief prayer. And that's it. People keep eating and talking. Whatever conversations, and there are literally hundreds of them, happen at tables among smaller groups. That's where the ministry happens too.

* * *

In the summer of 2012 the Presbyterian Church (USA) launched a new initiative, a commitment to start 1,001 "new worshiping communities" over the next ten years. The language was intentional, not just avoiding the word *church*, but with a stress on doing something *new*. Over halfway into the initiative, they are on their way.

When I visited with Vera White, who oversees the ministry, I asked how many of these new communities might be based around food in one way or another, dinner churches or something similar. She said that while they have been tracking all kinds of data, that wasn't a category on their radar. But she quickly added, while probably less than half were food-based, food is a prominent theme. She started naming some of those communities represented by the pins on the map, places like The Table in Casper, Wyoming; Isaiah's Table in Syracuse, New York; and Abundant Grace Dinner Church in West Windsor, New Jersey, near Princeton.

Vera was quick to point out that she and her colleagues don't use the word *model* when talking about these new communities because that implies some kind of conformity, when in reality no two of them are identical. They are each of them contextual, paying attention to the community in which the ministry will be planted.

Michael Frost and Alan Hirsch describe this as the difference between "attractional" and "incarnational" approaches to doing church. Attractional is what churches have mostly done, tried to find one more program to add on, one more feature to reach millennials or whomever. If we meet somewhere really cool, the thinking goes, they'll show up in droves. If we build it, they will come. That approach reminds me of a slick car salesperson who after way too many hours at his desk asks, "And what if I throw in floor mats? Would that do it?" Incarnational is more about simply being an authentic community, the kind of gathering people actually crave already.[4]

Among the food-based worship communities that Vera described, some of them eat the Eucharist around the meal, others enjoy a dinner together but don't really observe the Eucharist per se. For those who do, the liturgy can be very traditional and formal, and for others very casual. Some of these communities are focused on justice issues related to food, and so at the table there might be homeless persons, whereas other communities would go forth from their gatherings to practice ministries related to food insecurity.

Abundant Grace Dinner Church is one of those congregations Vera mentioned. They meet on Wednesday evenings in two different Presbyterian Churches in the suburbs of Princeton, New Jersey, the first and third Wednesdays at one and the second and fourth at another. They use the fellowship halls there free of charge, which is really nice since finances can be challenging for small dinner churches. Kristie Finley, the founding pastor, got the idea for a dinner church from her years as a minister to youth, where she claims she got all her good ideas. Actually, it's more complicated how the idea came to her and evolved over time.

Long before she went to Princeton Seminary as a second-career person, she worked with youth in her church, witnessing time and again how much bonding took place on mission trips in particular, everyone working and eating together. When she did go to seminary one of her professors assigned a project called "Change the World," the idea being to envision a way that parents might help shape youth early on, not wait for their adolescent years. Family meals were one obvious place. As a mother of four who loves to cook, the family meal was always valued in Kristie's home, their own "little Switzerland," as they called it, a neutral place where all ideas were welcome. That would become a hallmark of their dinner gatherings as church.

All of this came together when Kristie graduated and began her own bi-vocational ministry, a dinner church. She visited St. Lydia's Dinner Church, but put her own twist on how they gather. Recognizing how busy people are, the whole evening lasts an hour and a half at most, including prep time and the clean up afterwards.

The ten to twelve persons who gather (the ministry was only about a year old when I visited with her) participate in a typical kind of Presbyterian church service, but around tables. What I mean by typical is the Reformed pattern: call to worship, a prayer of confession, and typically a song or two, along with Scripture reading, and at the end a benediction. Kristie said she wasn't really comfortable being the person up front before a congregation the way ministers usually are, but this feels different because she usually offers some ideas from the Scripture reading, which everyone is encouraged to discuss throughout the meal. It's not so much a sermon as a meditation.

Very much like those earliest followers of Jesus and in a departure from the Reformed pattern, their dinner includes the breaking of bread before they eat and the cup afterwards. The bread is baked by one of the members and the cups afterwards are smaller ones filled with grape juice. After eating the bread as part of Communion (although I'm not sure they capitalize it), people are encouraged to continue eating it along with their soup. Some people drink the grape juice throughout the evening, but everyone's cup is refilled when it's time to resume the Communion. Of course the whole evening is communion.

Kristie hopes at some point to have a moveable feast, taking this ministry to nursing homes and the like, but always the whole worship experience, not just the meal. On their website (www.abundant.ministry-incubators.com), Kristie describes the weekly gatherings as "humble and simple, and beautiful." Such lovely words for a worship gathering.

* * *

Ben Johnston-Krase and Allen Brimer are Presbyterian ministers who went to seminary together in Chicago, where once a week they and two or three other couples got together to eat and enjoy each other's company. Part of the conversation always turned to the question, "What if we all lived on a farm together?" This wasn't a hippie kind of longing for Woodstock revisited, but more of an escapist dream at the time. It definitely wasn't the plans for someday planting Farm Church, at least not that any of them knew at the time.

But these families stayed in touch after graduating as each of them were called to different churches around the country. That staying in touch even included a retreat at Ghost Ranch in New Mexico back in 2014, where once again the idea of a farm came up. Not someone making a motion, "I move we start Farm Church. Is there a second?" No, nothing like that. It was more of a dream of being part of an intentional community.

Two weeks later, July 16, 2014, in the middle of the night Ben had a dream. He was being called to a church, except when the committee members hosting him took him to see the church building itself, there wasn't one. Just a farm. He woke up, the clock reading 3:17 AM, and Googled "Farm Church." Nothing, not really. He looked up the domain name and no one owned it. So he bought it right then and there. In the morning he told his wife about it, called Allen, some others in their small group of friends, and shared about the dream and, oh by the way, they own the domain now.

Since then the idea has sprouted and blossomed like seeds often do. Farm Church is located in Durham, North Carolina, a place with a foodie culture (great restaurants but also passion for locally grown crops and such), but more than that, a place with food insecurity. In a phrase, hungry people. In fact, Ben told me Farm Church's mission is very clear. It's about one thing, to leverage the resources to feed folks while also feeding each other as they gather as church. If that sounds like two things, they are wrapped up together in their minds. They now raise crops, not for profit, but to give them away to the hungry in the Durham area. The thirty to forty who attend most weeks include a lot of truly unchurched folks, some who were looking for something like this and others who weren't looking at all. But these folks were drawn to a congregation that dares put together these two words: *farm* and *church*.

While the dream is to someday own a farm just outside of town, right now they farm a smaller plot of land in town and meet at a building run by a non-profit there in Durham. On Sunday mornings folks arrive around 9:30 and are given tasks because there are always things to do on a farm—weeding, picking, feeding chickens, that sort of thing. Coffee is available of course, because what's church without coffee, right?

The really cool thing about starting the morning like this is that being in touch with the earth is being in touch with God. It's a gritty reminder that life is as ordinary as dirt and as sacred as living itself. That's why folks who are going about these chores hear someone nearby read a Psalm or voice some kind of "call to worship," a reminder that even in the field they have gathered in God's presence. That's worship as a way of life.

What happens when they are gathered for worship is very much what happens in lots of churches (singing, prayer, confession, and so forth), but always with a more organic feel, including the food they eat and the Eucharist too. Since they are just getting started as a church, so far people bring different foods, mostly healthy in nature. As for the Eucharist, Presbyterians don't usually eat it every Sunday, even if John Calvin had hoped for that, but Farm Church isn't your typical Presbyterian church. Ben told me they think about eating the Eucharist differently nearly every week, including letting folks at smaller tables say their own words of institution and breaking the bread, drinking from the cup, because all eating is sacred. Ben said he knows that's not the acceptable polity of Presbyterians, who usually insist that only ministers ordained in that tradition can preside at the table. But he's done worrying about those kinds of things. Sure, there are Sundays where he or Allen presides, but not always.

In a later email exchange, Ben reminded me of a quote by Frederick Buechner, "If we weren't blind as bats, we might see that life itself is sacramental." In that same book from which the quote comes, Buechner writes, "Needless to say, church isn't the only place where the holy happens. Sacramental moments can occur at any moment, at any place, and to anybody. Watching something get born. Making love. A walk on the beach. Somebody coming to see you when you're sick. A meal with people you love. Looking into a stranger's eyes and finding out they are not a stranger's."[5] All I can say to that is what I repeat after reading pretty much everything Buechner ever wrote and what I felt after visiting with Ben: "Amen."

* * *

Root and Branch is the name of another congregation that does dinner church, although they only do it twice a month on Sunday evenings with the other two Sunday worship services taking place in the mornings. Neil Ellington and Tim Kim are co-pastors in the Disciples of Christ tradition who met in seminary and wanted to plant a church together, although they didn't really know anything about the dinner church movement. It was Andrew Packman, another student at the University of Chicago Divinity School where they attended, who introduced them to the idea. Later, Neil became friends with Emily Scott, who started St. Lydia's in New York City, and who was very generous in sharing things that worked for them and didn't. Neil and Tim started scheming in 2012 and in the spring of 2013 launched their church.

Their humor and irreverent joking is contagious, even on the church's website. Neil's page describes him as currently building a house out of WWJD ankle bracelets, the point being that Root and Branch's dinner model is not an old way of doing church. While the Sunday morning gatherings are more vertical, meeting in an experimental theatre they rent, the dinner church gatherings take place on Sunday evenings in a cooking school where they rent space. Interestingly, they started with the dinner church idea, and only later ventured into the other kind of service on Sunday mornings as they recognized the need for higher energy gatherings, including more music, longer sermons, and less participation than required in dinner churches. Some of the regulars like one more than the other, but most folks who are part of their community see it as a package deal, a congregation that every other Sunday does something different.

Their dinner church gatherings typically have anywhere from thirty to fifty people in attendance, most of them in their twenties and thirties. Some are refugees from bad church experiences years ago, others with little to no church background, and all sorts of people in between, but all of them hungry for authentic community. Like most dinner churches the bread and cup bracket the meal, one they prepare together beforehand. The time of Communion is less formal than that at St. Lydia's, in part because of Tim and Neil's own eucharistic theology and background, but also because it feels more consistent with the casual atmosphere of a meal. When they break the bread, for instance, instead of the usual words about this being Christ's body broken for us, they say, "This is our body." (This reminds me of the minister who told me he still says, "This is my body" when breaking the bread, but looking up at the people, motioning to them. The folks gathered are Christ's body, his church.)

After supper, when the folks at Root and Branch partake of the cup those present can choose between grape juice and wine, and with both available not just during the time of Communion, but throughout the whole meal. Neil said that so far drunkenness hasn't been an issue.

As for a lot of dinner churches, finances are an issue. Neil and Tim are both less than full-time, more than part-time. Neil admitted to some anxiety since denominational funding can't go on indefinitely. But he also feels confident in what they are doing, something very much akin to how those earliest followers gathered in Jesus' name. His enthusiasm is contagious.

* * *

Or there's Simple Church in Grafton, Massachusetts, a United Methodist ministry about an hour west of Boston, depending on the traffic. Simple Church is a dinner church that's, well, simple. Zach Kerzee, the founding pastor, is a Texan like me who said he could talk all day about anything, but especially his love for a simple way of doing church. We talked by phone for an hour or more. Months later my wife and I visited the church in person.

By "simple," Zach means a minimalist approach to life as part of he and his wife's spirituality, not owning more than is needed, being part of the land, that sort of thing. Applied to their church, it means no printed bulletins because while those can help worshipers follow along, it's also one more piece of trash to throw away. Besides, worshipers don't really need bulletins because the evening's flow at their church is simple: they eat a meal together and talk, the bread and cup surrounding the meal. Even when eating the

Eucharist, they don't really draw on formal historic lingo, Zach usually riffing instead on a theme of the night, an image or idea from the Scriptures they read together. The Thursday night we were there, he pointed out it was a Thursday when Jesus ate that last meal with his friends. Unlike Dinner Church at St. Lydia's in Brooklyn, gatherings at Simple Church are simpler, at least in terms of the liturgy.

The idea for a dinner church was planted in Zach while in seminary at Harvard Divinity School. Thursday nights a bunch of the students would cram into someone's apartment to eat together and talk theology way into the night. (Ah, the good life.) He wondered why church couldn't be like this, stimulating and intimate, and over a meal. The church he was serving while in seminary was traditional in many ways, including a big building with less than ten in attendance most weeks. Zach said churches all across the northeast were closing left and right, and still are.

When he graduated and was appointed to another church, the one in Grafton, they sold the building and the proceeds became seed money for this new start. They kept the parsonage, a house located on farmland, which turned out to be a godsend. Zach figured they should do something with that land. He met the farmer whose land butted up to theirs and before long found himself working on the farm two to three hours a day a few days a week. He still does. As a result, the food grown there is donated to the church that eats together on Thursday evenings, much like he did with his friends in seminary.

When he started out he figured he would need to grow the church quickly because as with a lot of church starts, denominations underwrite these starts, but only for so long. The clock was ticking, so to speak, because the United Methodist powers-that-be gave him three years to be self-sustaining. And the thing took off from the start, forty or so folks showing up right away. So they divided and started a Friday night version too. The idea was to eventually host five dinner parties a week, forty at each. That way he would have a church of 200 but keep the intimacy factor. Except a winter even more snowy than usual for Massachusetts conspired against them, and before long they were back to Thursday nights only. Even with a simple approach to life (no building, no printing expenses, etc.), it would need to be self-sustaining at some point, and sooner rather than later.

But as it turns out, they found another way to make ends meet. Cooperating with a jobs corps in the area, they now bake bread and sell it in two different farmers' markets. It's a ministry because it's a way to meet people, but it's also a stream of revenue. At first they sold something like sixty to seventy loaves a week. Now it's more like 100 per week in the winter and they hope during the summer months they can triple that. At a cost of $7 per loaf (trust me, this is really good artisan bread), the church raises enough money to pay his salary, the only expense they have. He's even looking to buy a commercial oven and put it in their garage so they can bake the bread themselves. Zach's an apprentice at a commercial bakery where he is learning the trade.

In his mind Zach always imagined thirty hipsters like himself gathered in his basement and calling the dinner party "church." Not exactly. They do indeed meet in his basement, or did until they outgrew it and so now they rent the fellowship hall from another church. And they do call these dinner gatherings "church," but not very many hipsters come. There are a few singles and couples in their twenties like him and his wife, but a bunch of kids and a bunch of older folks too. There's no real racial diversity but only because there's not much racial diversity in the community. In addition to the diversity of age, however, there's also an intentional welcoming of LGBT folks, making up about a fourth of the congregation. Even some persons who wouldn't even identify themselves as Christian come, including one Jew.

After visiting Simple Church, I think the largest takeaway for me was the diminutive size of Grafton, Massachusetts, population 17,000. I suspect most of us upon learning about the dinner church movement might picture urban city centers, or at least large suburban towns bordering larger cities. I think about this because so many of the seminary students I teach serve in small communities, but not so small that dinner churches wouldn't appeal. People everywhere eat, that is a fact. And people everywhere long for community.

Like Zach, I grew up in the Bible belt, so I remember that little ditty we cited with our hands folded, "Here's the church. Here's the steeple. Open the doors. See all the people." There was that other version too, the one where you kept your fingers crossed on the outside of your knuckles, and so when the doors opened, you asked, "Where are all the people?" Turns out, in some places they are around a table instead. Simple Church's website reads, "We don't have a steeple. We don't have pews. We have a table. We'll set a place for you." Sounds like church to me. And it certainly felt like church.

* * *

I should also mention the ministry of H. A. "Bud" Tillinghast, a retired United Methodist minister who has started two Facebook pages dedicated to the dinner church movement. In fact, that's the name of his pages, Dinner Church Movement. A couple of years ago someone recommended he read Alan Streett's book *Subversive Meals*, about the radically inclusive eucharistic practices of the first Christians. Bud and his wife were fascinated by what they read, then wondered if anyone was doing dinner church. He Googled it, and the rest is history. One of his Facebook pages is where he posts and blogs about the movement, whereas the other is open for anyone involved or interested in dinner churches to ask questions and offer support to one another. If you visit those pages, you'll get a sense of the movement's momentum. Like me, Bud is convinced God is doing something special in these dinner churches.

The Future of Emmaus

I started writing this book around the time we learned we would be grandparents, a lovely meal when the Christ showed up as well, our family's own little "road to Emma story." As I finish writing, so much has happened. Emma has a little sister, Olivia, and they are growing so fast. Of course eating and talking will be a part of them for the rest of their lives. They will walk into the dining room of their house, sitting down with their parents to all sorts of meals and conversations. They will walk into school cafeterias with their friends, all of whom will complain about the food even as they fellowship the way only kids do. They will probably go on dates someday, food being a big part of that. I hope more than anything they will walk into church, likely a very different gathering than many of us now recognize. What will church life look like having been to Emmaus? What is our future? What does the dinner church movement signal for the future of Christianity?

As I think about those different kinds of gatherings, I think about the four key traits of those early Christian meal gatherings—intimacy, inclusion, joy, and participation—traits that are all too often missing in worship today. In contrast to the intimacy those ancient symposiums promoted over a meal, we hardly seem to know each other, resulting in what Rodney Clapp calls the "separation of church and friendship." He claims the church may have a surprising new mission: "to establish a cultural space for the birth and supported practice of friendship."[6] So many of the people we see at church are complete strangers to us. And eating together, as we have seen, is one of the best ways to foster intimacy and authentic community. As Leonard Sweet points out, the first command of God in the garden is "eat freely" (Gen 2:16), and the last command in Revelation is "drink freely" (Rev 22:17). Sweet says everything in between is a table where we eat with God and each other.[7]

And we are not very inclusive in our congregations either, with Sunday morning still being the most segregated time of the week. Except it's not just race but political views, sexual orientation, even lifestyle. Have you heard of Cowboy Church? It's for people who drive trucks and like country music, a church where people can gather with like-minded folks. I understand trying to reach different people groups, but must we segregate ourselves in the process? Are there churches for left-handed people too? What about golfer church? Left-handed golfer church? Would someone please inform the ministers starting churches that we're not all cowboys, surfers, art lovers, Frisbee throwers, or hipsters? This, I think, is what sets the dinner church movement apart from so many other innovations in ministry. *Everyone* eats. Maybe not vegan, organic, or local, but everyone eats.

In terms of joy, our churches seem fairly festive overall, although maybe "happy" is more accurate than "joyful," joking around and doing funny skits. Regardless, when it comes time to eat this meal we are definitely not joyful. More like a funeral. And then there's the participation that those first Christians enjoyed. Each person had something to contribute. When I go to church now, I am shocked at just how passive people are, even (or is it especially so?) in contemporary styles. Sure the band is playing, but the people often just listen to the guitar riffs and lead singers, or what have you. Is contributing our ears enough? Definitely not.

I do think two changes would be easy enough in most congregations. First, whether in a store front or grand old sanctuary we could celebrate a joyful Eucharist, passing the peace and playing festive music as people ate. We could eat it more often too, something that is happening in lots of places, a kind of eucharistic revival. I sometimes hear people say that their church doesn't eat it every Sunday so that it's more special when they do. I usually reply, "And do you feel that way about meals at home?" I'm guessing that for most folks dinner is a regular thing, not once a month. And I've never seen a church apply the "more special" theory to the sermon or offering, things that happen every Sunday.

Second, we could also practice more inclusion at the table, opening it up to children, to seekers, to anyone who comes, even inviting our unchurched friends. These are baby steps that could make a big difference. But those other two traits—the intimacy of a full meal and meaningful participation—are going to be harder to pull off, unless it's in small groups or small churches.

* * *

As far as I'm concerned, the best piece about worship outside of the Bible is Annie Dillard's essay, "An Expedition to the Pole." A few lines here and there get quoted on occasion, but the whole thing is pure genius. I have my students in seminary read it, typically resulting in two responses: those who love it and those who might if they understood it. That's partly because it's a parable of sorts, an extended comparison between what happens in worship on any given Sunday and some polar expeditions in the nineteenth and early twentieth centuries, what she calls searching for the "pole of great price." In one paragraph she describes attending a Catholic mass, only to tell stories about explorers in the next. Like the parables of Jesus, the essay demands our best thinking.

She describes, for instance, a Sunday service when no one could find the opening hymn, not even the organist. How instead of a sermon proclaiming gospel, there were mostly announcements, including one about how the acolyte would be lighting the two Advent candles momentarily, only the candles were already lit. She continues, "During communion, the priest handed me a wafer which proved to be stuck to five other wafers. I waited while he tore the clump into rags of wafer, resisting the impulse to help."[8] Dillard notes that high school stage plays are more polished than our church services. She's got that right. She adds, we are like dancing bears in the circus, clumsy and sure to fall down.

When detailing polar expeditions, she lists for example the famous Franklin expedition of 1845, which instead of bringing along additional coal should they run out of fuel, "made room for a 1,200-volume library, 'a hand-organ, playing fifty tunes,' china place settings for officers and men, cut-glass wine goblets, and sterling silver flatware."[9] Seriously? Books and silverware for an arctic exploration? Of course as readers we are supposed to imagine how churches do something similar when it comes to traditions in worship.

Dillard describes tourists and crew alike on the deck of a ship, enjoying coffee and doughnuts, completely oblivious that no one is at the helm while we float past icebergs that could rip the hull into pieces and plunge us into the icy waters. In the most quoted part of her essay, she writes, "The churches are children playing on the floor with their chemistry sets, mixing up a batch of TNT to kill a Sunday morning. It is madness to wear ladies' straw hats and velvet hats to church; we should all be wearing crash helmets."[10]

Because the essay is a parable, there are lots of insights to be gleaned. For me, two things stand out. First, I recognize the craziness of this journey called worship, daring to sail toward the mystery of God; and second, still we set off each week because God has planted a longing in our hearts. We always have set off to worship. Some of us always will. But what will these worship experiences look like?

* * *

As I think about the future of the church, let me go on record as saying I have never been very good at predicting the future of anything. My March Madness brackets for college basketball each spring are usually busted after the first round, second round at best. If you had asked me as a kid to predict how we would travel in the future, I would definitely have voted for flying cars. Turns out, our Fords and Nissans will still hug the road, only without us at the wheel, so to speak. Self-driving cars; I never saw that coming.

So when people ask me about the future of church, I usually start with a disclaimer, that I'm not very good at predictions. After that, here's what I venture: there will always be big churches, too big to fail, as the experts said of some financial institutions during the recession of 2008. Where I grew up in Texas there are churches so large they have bowling alleys and dry cleaners within their walls. Seriously. Garrison Keillor refers to those places as "Six Flags over Jesus." That might be a little harsh, but it's likely those congregations will survive any kind of cultural shifts. Will they promote small groups more and more? I hope so, especially eucharistic ones.

What concerns me about the future are the not-so-big churches, the middle size and smaller, maybe the middle size most of all since at least the smallest ones are potentially nimbler. So many congregations are already diminishing in numbers, and the denominational leaders know this, many of them suffering from insomnia I'm sure. The math is simple: so many gray heads on a Sunday, minus those who die each year, adding back in those who join, and in many places, well, the tally moves toward zero. Although I question the number, I read in *The Christian Century* that on average as many as ten churches close permanently every day in America.[11] This much I do know, overwhelming numbers of young people are not flocking toward churches. In the last decade nearly 700,000 people have left religion, "the only group posting numeric gains in all fifty states." The "nones" (as in no religious affiliation) and the "dones" (as in "we are done with this kind of church") have voted with their feet.[12]

All across this country, congregations close every week, have one final service, then padlock the door. I preached at one in Kansas City years ago, their last time together. Very sad. And recently a church I formerly served as pastor voted to close their doors. This happened in Great Britain and Europe a century or so ago, except at least those unused buildings are historic, worth touring and taking snapshots of.[13] I doubt seriously that a former United Methodist church of 220 people in, say, Des Moines, Iowa, will be preserved for tours. The same for a former Lutheran congregation in the suburbs of Sacramento or wherever.

Over lunch, my good friend Teresa Stewart pointed out how many small churches operate out of pathology, comparing themselves to the big guys down the street, when in reality small churches have so many advantages. She's right, of course. What could happen is that a number of micro-churches could spring up. We know micro-breweries, all the craze in some places. What about a small church gathering? There'd be no tours the way breweries offer because maybe these congregations will meet in a storefront, or in a restaurant, but there could be thriving congregations.

Honestly, when I graduated from seminary in the mid-1980s, I had grander visions of ministry. If I were going to serve a church, it would be big and stately, large enough to feed my ego and ensure that my retirement nest egg would suffice. Back then the term "bivocational minister" signaled failure in my mind, someone who either wasn't gifted enough for larger congregations or who was headed back to some place like Wyoming where the deer and antelope not only played but also outnumbered the people and therefore had small churches. A bi-vocational minister was a rancher and part-time preacher who didn't have near enough time to study for Sunday's sermon or to read the latest book by Frederick Buechner or Barbara Brown Taylor, assuming these part-timers had even heard of them. Sad, I know, but that was my way of thinking.

What's even sadder, there are remnants of that thought pattern still hovering in my head somewhere, no matter how hard I try to stifle them. Slowly but surely though my thinking is changing; and our thinking will have to keep changing. I suspect ministers in the future will have no choice but to be bi-vocational, as they put food on the table and help folks gather around another table a few evenings a night. The bivocational ministers at Community Dinners in Seattle receive only one-seventh of a salary since they only gather one night a week and have full-time jobs the rest of the week.

But bi-vocational ministry raises justice questions. If a person graduates with a bachelor's degree, she/he can go get a job, making a decent living while paying off whatever student loans piled up. But what if we ask that person to get a seminary degree after college as well, piling on even more debt, only to still work that first job, and oh by the way, serve a church part-time? Smaller congregations really are going to have to wrestle with this. I have a dream that seminaries will find generous donors who understand the justice issues and who will enable ministers to attend seminary for free. If someone reading this wants to write a check to Saint Paul School of Theology, the seminary where I teach, fine with me. I'm sure our students would be thrilled.

I also think that finding the right *kind* of paying job will be key. A barista and minister seem more compatible to me than a plumber and pastor, but that's my own bias. I once visited a lovely little independent bookstore in Boston that also doubled as a bakery. I was pretty sure one of those was more lucrative than the other. What if a pastor not only met with several small clusters for eucharistic dinner parties in the evenings but also ran a bakery of her own? What if the church felt more like a bakery or bookstore than what we currently associate with the word *church*? After all, bakeries and bookstores are often much more welcoming than some churches.

* * *

On Tuesday, October 31, 2017, Lutherans and Catholics will gather to commemorate the 500th anniversary of the Reformation. The meeting will be too large for the little town of Wittenburg, the original site of Luther's ninety-five theses, so they will gather instead in Lund, Sweden, for what is one of those truly rare moments in church history. I can imagine historians 500 years from now looking back on this event, although who knows how they will view it. No one can say for sure what the church's future looks like, not just in the next 500 years but the next five for that matter. But if that math is correct, that Christianity has a rummage sale every half a millennium or so, our Communion practices should definitely be on the list of items to rethink right now. This was certainly the case at each of the previous 500-year marks in our history, with Communion front and center in debates and discussions.

As I have pondered the image of the church's rummage sale, I have thought about the few garage sales my wife and I endured before Craigslist came along. We'd pull the stuff out of storage and put stickers with prices on all of it. A dollar for this, and five dollars for that. Old tennis rackets, a bicycle pump, kids' puzzles, the usual stuff. But garage sales can be painful, and not just in terms of sheer endurance, sitting on the driveway for the better part of a Saturday morning. No, I mean how letting things go hurts. When we moved my mother from Texas to Missouri, I sold every piece of furniture in record time, thanks to Craigslist. What I didn't stop to ponder fully was how hard that must have been on her, watching all that furniture disappear into the back of pickups and U-Hauls, never to be seen again. She had worked most her adult life as a single mother to provide a home and furnish it.

There is pain associated with change, no doubt, and changes in our worship patterns are often near the top of the list. But perhaps another image associated with garage sales could provide some comfort. My wife and I have sold furniture over the years, as have most folks; and yes, it's painful to see that couch we loved, the one the kids thought was a trampoline, now marked down to $75, or that dining room table where the kids first learned to eat and where we told stories reduced to $30 because it has seen better days. This is all true. But what if we focused on what we plan to do with the money, how we are in the market for new seating and a new table?

What if the pews we have loved are now replaced with chairs so that we can actually see one another? And what if the small rectangular table up front in our churches is being replaced with a larger round one that we can sit around? The poet Chuck Lathrop writes, "But the times and the tables are changing and rearranging."[14] Those are true words.

If Phyllis Tickle is right about what happens when new worship forms emerge, then there are reasons to be optimistic about the church in general, not just dinner churches. She lists three likely outcomes, "First, a new, more vital form of Christianity does indeed emerge." Second, the current expression that had been dominant "is reconstituted into a more pure and less ossified expression," and third, the faith spreads to people who were not being reached previously.[15]

* * *

Despite my lover's quarrel with the church, I share Tickle's optimism. If anything, I'm excited about what might come about as we rethink Communion and community. At the beginning of this book I cited a quote from Susan Marks, "A book about meals is a book about magic—the magical transformation of people into the identities constructed by the foods they ingest, the group they dine with, and the ideas they share at their gatherings."[16] There really is something magical about meals.

RSVP is the natural culmination of a book that began with an invitation, much like first-century banquets began with formal invites. In this case you were invited to join me on a journey, back in time, to look around at what God is doing right now, and into the church's future. For your coming along, I am grateful beyond words. In some ways reading this book was your RSVP, although it seems to me the invitation is more long-term than that, more open-ended, imagining a future church that you are invited not only to attend but help shape.

Pondering what such a church might look like, I'm reminded of a wonderful quote that, if you will indulge me, has more to say about Christian community than you might think at first. It also echoes Dillard's imagery of an expedition. Here's the quote: "If you want to build a ship, don't drum up people to collect wood and don't assign them tasks and work, but rather teach them to long for the endless immensity of the sea."[17] Applied to church, maybe the key is to teach people (or maybe just find people who already know what it means) to long for the endless immensity of God who is to be found in a community gathered around tables. When we are gathered together like that, as Luke tells it in his story about the road to Emmaus, the Christ keeps showing up and breaking bread with us. And at the table our eyes are opened.

APPENDIX

Different Words of Institution

New Frames for Introducing the Jesus Meal

There's no use pretending otherwise, in most churches on any given Sunday when it's time to eat the Jesus meal, the setting brought to mind is the upper room the night before Jesus dies. That is the church's default way for framing the story of Communion. The lights are sometimes lowered, a musician plays somber music, and the person presiding highlights Jesus' suffering and death. That highlighting happens via *words of institution*, the traditional name for a story that begins, "the Lord Jesus on the night when he was betrayed took a loaf of bread . . ." (1 Cor 11:23). Those words of institution serve as the narrative frame for the meal, a chapter in the plot of the gospel story. But here's the problem. While that sort of narrative frame makes perfect sense during Holy Week, it doesn't have to be the default frame for every Sunday, especially in light of so many other themes associated with the Jesus meal in Scripture.

At least seven other stories and images in the New Testament could be employed on any given Sunday, Scripture passages that resonate more fully with a meal characterized by those four traits of intimacy, inclusion, joy, and participation. In planning for such gatherings and choosing between these many options, much would depend on the theme of the day arising from the Scriptures. As we look at these different passages, I'll suggest language we might use in our gatherings when moving to the table, different words of institution.[1]

Feedings in the Wilderness

The feeding of the multitudes is the only miracle performed by Jesus found in all four Gospels. I realize we looked at it earlier, but the church has rarely taken seriously the prominence of this story. With Matthew and Mark telling two versions, we have six different accounts, none of them identical and yet all of them using the words we typically associate with the Jesus meal. This is a passage worthy of more attention and one that could frame our feasting in worship, especially with its justice theme of feeding the poor and outcasts.

For example, in Matthew's two accounts, the first one takes place in Jewish territory when Jesus feeds 5,000 (Matt 14:13–21). That's where Jesus' ministry largely happens in Matthew, among the Jews. What we often miss is that the second version, the one where he feeds 4,000, happens in Gentile territory, and this after his encounter with a Canaanite woman who challenges Jesus' worldview (Matt 15:21–28) when he calls her a dog. If you don't know the story, look it up. As my kids would say, it's a hot mess.

I could imagine a couple different ways of framing the Jesus meal using these two stories. If a worship service and sermon focused on matters of food insecurity or similar themes, rather than framing the meal with the traditional language of "On the night when he was betrayed . . . ," what if the person celebrating said something like this:

> When Jesus looked out on the poor and hungry, he had compassion for them and called his disciples to feed them. He took bread, blessed it, broke it, and gave it to them. Jesus gathers us together, feeding us, and calling us to feed the hungry. We eat in remembrance of him. We drink this cup as well, as part of a new covenant, remembering the poor among us, remembering Jesus.

Or if the gathering focused on crossing boundaries, on being an inclusive church, maybe something like this:

> When Jesus looked out on the poor and hungry, it was not just Jews like himself, but he had compassion on the Gentiles, those who were different, those who were thought of as "other." He took bread, gave thanks, broke it, and gave it to all. We eat in remembrance of Jesus whose love is for all persons, including the marginalized. We drink this cup as well, part of a new covenant for all persons.

The Bread of Heaven and True Vine

John's Gospel does not tell the same upper room story as the first three Gospels, highlighting instead Jesus washing the disciples' dirty feet, modeling servanthood (John 13). But not surprisingly, there are eucharistic references elsewhere in the Fourth Gospel. For example, Jesus encounters a woman from Samaria, a passage that scholars suggest echoes themes of courtship in the Old Testament, stories where a man meets a woman at a well. This particular woman has three strikes against her, so to speak. She is a woman in a man's world, a Samaritan in a Jewish world, and has had five husbands. On that last count, the traditional interpretation is that she is some kind of loose woman, but in fact women did not file for divorce in the first century. This woman has been abandoned five times for whatever reason. As John tells the story, Jesus comes courting, not in a romantic sort of way, and yet offering her a drink that brings eternal life (John 4). Given her situation, I can only imagine how "thirsty" she must have been. Or how about a few chapters later in John's gospel when he calls himself "the bread of life," a bread that satisfies our deepest hungers (John 6). In John 15, he calls himself "the true vine" (John 15:1). Presiding at the table we might offer words like these:

> In John's gospel, Jesus said he is the bread of life, that whoever eats this bread will never be hungry, that whoever trusts in him will never be thirsty. Today we eat this bread and drink this cup, remembering that it is God who meets our needs, who fills us up. We feast in Jesus' name.

Jesus Feeding Peter

We looked earlier at the last story in John's gospel, the one where Peter who denied Jesus is now fed, a meal of mercy and grace to be sure. Forgiveness is one of those themes often highlighted in Lord's Supper services, except usually emphasizing sin and confession more than celebrating the forgiveness we have in Christ. While a worship gathering might have a time of confession before the meal, at the table we eat a meal of forgiveness. This is yet another wonderful reason to celebrate a festive Eucharist. Given that kind of focus, the person presiding at the table might offer words like these:

When Jesus restored Peter, assuring him of God's forgiveness, he did so over a meal by the seashore. Jesus calls us to this feast as the forgiven people of God. We eat this bread and drink this cup in celebration of God's restoring love and grace. We are indeed forgiven. Let us feast.

Feasting in Emmaus

As we considered at length earlier, this is one of the great eucharistic stories in all the New Testament. Two disciples, Cleopas and his traveling companion, have yet to recognize the resurrection of Jesus, that he has conquered death. At a table in their home, Jesus the invited guest becomes the host, and their eyes are opened. This story could be a powerful one when taking Communion to those unable to attend church services. But even at a table in our gatherings, the person presiding could share words of resurrection joy like these:

> When Jesus journeyed with the couple on the road to Emmaus, their hearts burned within them, even if they didn't recognize him. At the table in their home he feasted with them, taking bread, giving thanks, breaking it, and giving it to them. Then their eyes were opened. At this table we eat bread and recognize the resurrected Jesus among us. We drink this cup to celebrate his presence.

The Early Community in Acts

Because the book of Acts is a long and involved story, every once in a while Luke offers readers a summary. The first of those summaries, in Acts 2, highlights several characteristics of that community of Jesus' followers, what we would eventually refer to as the church. Here's the passage:

> They devoted themselves to the apostles' teaching and fellowship, to the breaking of bread and the prayers. Awe came upon everyone, because many wonders and signs were being done by the apostles. All who believed were together and had all things in common; they would sell their possessions and goods and distribute the proceeds to all, as any had need. Day by day, as they spent much time together in the temple, they broke bread at home and ate their food with glad and generous hearts, praising God and having the

goodwill of all the people. And day by day the Lord added to their number those who were being saved (Acts 2:42–47).

"Their food" of course refers to the ordinary food of their evening meal, whereas the phrase *breaking bread* is Luke's expression for the meal we now call Communion. But Luke also highlights how they devoted themselves to "fellowship," the life they shared together over that evening meal and a commitment to care for each other's needs. These too are things we might highlight when celebrating at the table, perhaps with words like these:

> When the earliest followers of Jesus experienced the Spirit's coming at Pentecost, breaking bread was one of the hallmarks of their gatherings. They ate their meals together as well as the bread and wine. They devoted themselves to sharing life together and caring for each other. Today we feast on this meal as brothers and sisters in Christ, celebrating the Spirit of God among us.

Paul and the Sailors in Acts

We looked at this story in some detail in an earlier chapter, recalling the radically open table with room for all persons to join the feast of God. Sermons and worship services focusing on inclusion could lead to using words of institution something like this:

> When Paul was on a ship, he offered this bread to the sailors and Roman soldiers on board, people considered far from God. He said it was for their salvation, so that they might be made whole. He took bread, gave thanks to God, broke it, and gave it to them. Today we eat this meal, a meal for all persons who would "taste and see that God is good" (Ps 30). This is the bread of life and this is the cup of salvation for all God's children.

Feasting at the Messianic Banquet

The book of Revelation certainly strikes fear in the heart of many a reader, but mostly in those passages sandwiched between the seven letters to the churches in the early chapters (Rev 2–3) and those latter ones describing the New Jerusalem, what some call John's vision of the resurrected life (Rev 19–21). The middle section is indeed intimidating; but not John's final vision where we read about the banquet of God, when the church which is God's bride sits down with Christ the groom. With the image of heaven as banquet, a service on our future hope might lead to words like these spoken at the table:

> In the book of Revelation, John describes a great banquet, the marriage supper of the Lamb, the church as Jesus' bride. He declares that blessed are those who have been invited. When we eat this meal of bread and wine, we remember the resurrected Jesus who is with us now, but also his promise to eat with us at the heavenly banquet. This bread and wine are a foretaste of a great heavenly banquet, a place where will be no more "mourning and crying and pain." We feast in anticipation of that day.

Recommended Reading

Bahnson, Fred. *Soil and Sacrament: A Spiritual Memoir of Food and Faith.* New York: Simon and Schuster, 2013.

Banks, Robert J. *Paul's Idea of Community: The Early House Churches in Their Cultural Setting.* Rev. ed. Grand Rapids: Baker Academic, 2012.

Bass, Diana Butler. *Grounded: Finding God in the World: A Spiritual Revolution.* New York: HarperOne, 2015.

Boin, Douglas. *Coming Out Christian in the Roman World: How the Followers of Jesus Made a Place in Caesar's Empire.* New York: Bloomsbury, 2015.

Boulton, Matthew Myer. *God Against Religion: Rethinking Christian Theology through Worship.* Grand Rapids: Eerdmans, 2008.

Brock, Rita Nakashima and Parker, Rebecca Ann. *Saving Paradise: How Christianity Traded Love of This World for Crucifixion and Empire.* Boston: Beacon, 2008.

Crossan, John Dominic. *The Birth of Christianity: Discovering What Happened in the Years Immediately after the Execution of Jesus.* New York: HarperSanFrancisco, 1998.

Ehrenreich, Barbara. *Dancing in the Streets: A Collective History of Joy.* New York: Picador, 2006.

Frost, Michael, and Alan Hirsch. *The Shaping of Things to Come: Innovation and Mission in the 21st Century.* Rev. ed. Grand Rapids: Baker, 2013.

Honoré, Carl. *In Praise of Slowness: Challenging the Cult of Speed*. New York: HarperSanFrancisco, 2004.

Karris, Robert J. *Eating Your Way through Luke's Gospel*. Collegeville, MN: Liturgical, 2006.

Kreglinger, Gisela H. *The Spirituality of Wine*. Grand Rapids: Eerdmans, 2016.

Lathrop, Gordon W. *The Four Gospels on Sunday: The New Testament and the Reform of Christian Worship*. Minneapolis: Fortress, 2012.

McGowan, Andrew B. *Ancient Christian Worship: Early Church Practices in Social, Historical, and Theological Perspective*. Grand Rapids: Baker Academic, 2014.

Meeks, Wayne A. *The First Urban Christians: The Social World of the Apostle Paul*. 2nd ed. New Haven, CT: Yale University Press, 2003.

Miles, Sara. *Take This Bread: The Spiritual Memoir of a Twenty-First Century Christian*. New York: Ballantine, 2008.

Pollan, Michael. *Cooked: A Natural History of Transformation*. New York: Penguin, 2013.

Rice, Charles L. *The Embodied Word: Preaching as Art and Liturgy*. Minneapolis: Fortress, 1991.

Smith, C. Christopher, and John Pattison. *Slow Church: Cultivating Community in the Patient Way of Jesus*. Downer's Grove, IL: InterVarsity, 2014.

Smith, Dennis E. *From Symposium to Eucharist: The Banquet in the Early Christian World*. Minneapolis: Fortress, 2003.

Smith, Dennis E., and Hal E. Taussig. *Many Tables: The Eucharist in the New Testament and Liturgy Today*. Eugene, OR: Wipf and Stock, 2001.

Sparks, Paul, Tim Soerens, and Dwight J. Friesen. *The New Parish: How Neighborhood Churches Are Transforming Mission, Discipleship, and Community*. Downer's Grove, IL: InterVarsity, 2014.

Stookey, Laurence Hull. *Eucharist: Christ's Feast with the Church*. Nashville: Abingdon, 1993.

Streett, R. Alan. *Subversive Meals: An Analysis of the Lord's Supper under Roman Domination during the First Century*. Eugene, OR: Pickwick, 2013.

Suttle, Tim. *Shrink: Faithful Ministry in a Church-Growth Culture*. Grand Rapids: Zondervan, 2014.

Taussig, Hal E. *In the Beginning was the Meal: Social Experimentation and Early Christian Identity*. Minneapolis: Fortress, 2009.

Tickle, Phyllis. *The Great Emergence: How Christianity Is Changing and Why*. Grand Rapids: Baker, 2008.

Volf, Miroslav, and Justin E. Crisp, eds. *Joy and Human Flourishing: Essays on Theology, Culture, and the Good Life*. Minneapolis: Fortress, 2015.

Wirzba, Norman. *Food and Faith: A Theology of Eating*. Cambridge: Cambridge University, 2011.

Witherington, Ben III. *Making a Meal of It: Rethinking the Theology of the Lord's Supper*. Waco, TX: Baylor University Press, 2008.

Acknowledgments

If you are ever fortunate enough to visit the Holy Land, the birthplace of the Jews and Jesus, don't just count your blessings; it wouldn't hurt to learn a few key phrases as well in preparation for the journey. Expressions like "Good morning," "Good night," and "Please" come to mind. But for me, the most important phrase in any language has to be, "Thank you." So, for instance, when your Israeli tour guide points out where the restroom is located after a long bus ride, in Hebrew you would say, *Toda*, accent on the last syllable. For a safe arrival at the various pilgrimage sites, you might offer thanks to your Palestinian bus driver with the Arabic word, *Shukran*.

Among my friends who don't really claim to know another language, they usually are familiar with the Spanish word *"Gracias,"* like when their enchiladas arrive or the waiter brings more chips and hot sauce. That's close to the Italian, of course, which is *"Grazie."* In Germany the most common way to say thanks is *"Danke."* In Japan you say *"Arigato."* And for a lovely baguette in France *"Merci,"* another somewhat familiar expression.

But my favorite word for thanks is the Greek word, in part because it's such a beautiful word, at least to my ears; but also because it is the language of the New Testament. The Greek word for thanks is *"eucharisto,"* literally the first-person, singular verb, "I give thanks." *Eucharisto* might seem familiar to some readers since used as a noun (eucharistia) it is the earliest name for the meal Christians everywhere eat in remembrance of Jesus, the Eucharist, a meal of bread and wine, a meal of thanksgiving.

There are a number of people I wish to thank who contributed to the writing of this volume, including: Dennis Smith, Teresa Williams, Joanna Harader, David May, Joanna Chenoweth, Teresa Stewart, Bud Tillinghast, Wendie Brockhaus, Robert Fugarino, Dawn Weaks, Young Ho Chun, Randy Irey, Bill Stancil, and David May , all of whom read drafts or listened to me drone on at different times. A special thanks also to my student assistant

Angie McNeil for her computer skills and perseverance, my friend David Firman who designed my web page (www.drmikegraves.com) and offered to become my publicist, and lastly, my editor, Rodney Clapp. I should buy you all dinner some time. How does bread and wine sound?

I'm also grateful to the ministers of various dinner churches who agreed to host me and/or have a conversation via phone: Emily Scott, Vera White, Verlon Fosner, Ben Johnston-Krase, Allen Brimer, Alex Raabe, Zach Kersee, Neil Ellington, and Kristie Finley. There were probably others, and if I've missed someone, I'm so sorry.

I also wish to offer thanks to my faculty colleagues and the board of trustees at Saint Paul School of Theology who granted me a study leave in the fall of 2015. For these colleagues and friends who leant me support, and for you the reader joining me in this exploration, I offer my thanks. *Eucharisto*!

Notes

Introduction: An Invitation

1. Schmemann, *Life of the World,* 16.

2. I think especially about Schlosser, *Fast Food Nation,* and the chapter on the "slow food" movement in Honoré, *Praise of Slowness,* 53–84.

3. McGowan, *Ancient Christian Worship,* 19.

4. Some readers will recognize this as the title of a book by the sixteenth-century Reformer Martin Luther, a collection of sayings he shared over food and drink. What I have in mind is inspired by a much older work, Plutarch's first-century reflections on dinner parties.

5. Tickle, *Great Emergence,* 16. Tickle credits Angelican bishop Mark Dyer with the line about every 500 years.

6. Smith, *Symposium to Eucharist,* 147–49, notes that any fixed *seder* practices would not have developed until at least the second century into the third century. See also Barth, *Rediscovering the Lord's Supper,* 10.

7. Newman, *Essay on the Development of Christian Doctrine.* Originally published in 1878, Newman compares doctrinal developments to how a seed needs time to germinate or how a river's course evolves over time. Whether those changes are good or bad must continually be considered.

8. Sweet, *Tablet to Table,* 114.

9. Pollan, *Cooked,* 5–7. A special thanks to Ginger Rothhaas, one of my students who pointed me to the Netflix documentary based on this book. What a treat.

10. Schmemann, *Life of the World,* 14–15.

11. Smith, *Symposium to Eucharist,* 285.

12. Greeley, *Catholic Imagination,* 4.

13. So far as we know, the noun form was not popularized until the early part of the second century in a document called *The Didache,* and later in the middle of the second century when Justin Martyr referred to it in his *Apology.*

Chapter 1: The Meal

1. I am drawing here from the works of several scholars, most notably, Meeks, *First Urban Christians*, 157–62; McGowan, *Ancient Christian Worship*, 19–64; and the classic work in the field, Smith, *Symposium to Eucharist*, 13–46. Interestingly, at roughly the same time Dennis Smith was writing his book in the States, German scholar Matthias Klinghardt came to almost identical conclusions in his own volume. If you read German, the title is *Gemeinschaftsmahl und Mahlgemeinschaft*. All these works draw from earlier articles and essays by each of them as well as others.

2. See Pervo's book by the same name, *Profit with Delight*.

3. Crossan, *Birth of Christianity*, 424, emphasis his.

4. Lathrop, *Four Gospels on Sunday*, 169.

5. Witherington III, *Making a Meal of It*, 137.

6. On this point, see Wirzba, *Food and Faith*, 27–29.

7. Gopnik, *Table Comes First*, 77. Michael Pollan comes to a similar conclusion in his book, *Cooked*.

8. Ibid, 9.

9. Smith, *Symposium to Eucharist*, 286.

10. Ehrenreich, *Dancing in the Streets*, 77.

11. Niequist, *Bread and Wine*, 232.

12. Kreglinger, *Spirituality of Wine*, 62–63.

13. Dillard, *Holy the Firm*, 63.

14. See Smith, *Symposium to Eucharist*, 6, who contends that Greco-Roman meals were more of a middle ground, sacred and secular. For a good overview of how Jewish tradition made no distinction between the two, see Frost and Hirsch, *Shaping of Things to Come*, 162–66.

15. Bass, *Grounded*, 120–21. Cox, *Future of Faith*, 2, suggests much the same thing with the phrase, "the spiritual *within* the secular" (emphasis his).

16. Norris, *Quotidian Mysteries*, 3.

17. Dillard, *For the Time Being*, 88.

18. Honoré, *In Praise of Slowness*, 54–55.

19. Smith and Pattison, *Slow Church*, 209.

20. Ehrenreich, *Dancing in the Streets*, 1–20, which notes a whole range of theories as to why humans crave joy.

21. For a different take on a third place approach to ministry, see Frost and Hirsch, *Shaping of Things to Come*, 99, who talk about a group of Christians in Australia who have started what they call Third Place Communities.

22. Smith, *Symposium to Eucharist*, 28.

23. See, for instance, Smith and Taussig, *Many Tables*. They make this point repeatedly throughout the volume.

24. Six different versions of the wilderness feedings can be found in the four Gospels, with two versions in Matthew and Mark, feedings of 5,000 and 4,000. They are: Matthew 14:15–1; Matthew 15:32–38; Mark 6:30–44; Mark 8:1–9; Luke 9:12–17; and John 6:5–13. The references in Luke's writings can be found in Luke 24:28–30 and Acts 27:27–36.

Chapter 2: The Guest List

1. Although originally Karris offered this insight in an earlier work (*Luke: Artist and Theologian*), a more accessible work is his book *Eating Your Way through Luke's Gospel*, 14.

2. For a more nuanced treatment of the Pharisees, see Levine, *Misunderstood Jew*. There is also the less accessible but more detailed treatment of Neusner and Chilton, eds., *In Quest of the Historical Pharisees*. Suffice it to say, few readers of the New Testament realize the Pharisees were not a monolithic group.

3. Parables don't really have names, and as scholars note, supplying a title often directs attention to one aspect of a parable that might not be primary. There's also no use of the word "prodigal" in the story itself.

4. Lathrop, *Four Gospels on Sunday*, 160–62, argues something similar.

5. Julier, *Eating Together*.

6. Crossan, *Jesus*, 69.

7. Wirzba, *Food and Faith*, 38, emphasis his.

8. Crossan, *Birth of Christianity*, 427–28, mentions these three types of dwellings using slightly different terminology and drawing on two works by Packer, "Housing," 80–95, and *Insulae of Imperial Ostia*.

9. Shelton, *As the Romans Did*, 81.

10. Ibid., 426.

11. Miles, *Take This Bread*.

12. Lathrop, *Four Gospels on Sunday*, 59.

13. The saying is credited to Barthes by a number of sources. See, for example, Fowler, *Let the Reader Understand*, 233.

14. Crossan, *Greatest Prayer*, 133.

15. Streett, *Subversive Meals*, claims that just as the first Passover protested Egyptian rule, the Jesus meal at Passover protested Roman domination. Some scholars have discredited some of his findings, claiming that he assigns too much historicity to the Gospel accounts. Even so, there is good evidence that the Gospel writers themselves would likely have protested Roman rule in their telling of the Jesus story.

16. Ibid., 133. See also Wright, "Joy," 57, who notes how celebrations of "Lord Jesus" often stood in contrast to celebrations of "Lord Caesar," Christian worship as a form of protest.

17. Boin, *Coming Out Christian in the Roman World*, 3.

18. Ibid., 5.

19. Meeks, *First Urban Christians*, 78–79. Meeks does think that given the use of different words that most clubs used to identify themselves the various Christian groups did not model themselves on the usual associations.

20. Smith, *Symposium to Eucharist*, 358–59. This is a footnote in which he engages Corley, *Private Women, Public Meals*, who has done extensive work on this passage in Luke.

21. See Standhartinger, "Women," 97.

22. Craddock, *Craddock Stories*, 28–29.

23. Suttle, *Shrink.*

24. Berry, *Jayber Crow*, 185, cited in Suttle, *Shrink*, 13.

25. Suttle, *Shrink,*14.

26. See for instance Scott, *Hear Then the Parable*, 373–87.

27. Suttle, *Shrink*, 47.

28. Howard Merritt, "Leading," 45. Merritt references comments about St. Lydia's Dinner Church by Stephanie Spellers, who oversees evangelism efforts on the part of the Episcopal Church.

29. See Smith, *Symposium to Eucharist*, 24, for his discussion of Plutarch.

30. Ibid., 25.

Chapter 3: The Ambiance

1. Smith, *Symposium to Eucharist*, 12, 284.

2. The older brother uses the word as well when he tells the father that he never even got a goat to eat with his friends so they might *celebrate* (Luke 15:29).

3. Ehrenreich, *Dancing in the Streets,* 18–19, shows how anthropologists have tended to "draw a line between *ritual* and *festivity*," the former being religious and the latter either "pagan, recreational, or for children" (emphasis hers).

4. Smith, *Symposium to Eucharist*, 12, 80.

5. James, *Varieties of Religious Experience*, 377–78, emphasis his. Pollan, *Cooked*, 398, cites James, noting as well the psychologist's overly optimistic embrace of alcohol.

6. Kreglinger, *Spirituality of Wine*, 98.

7. Welch was a Methodist minister who not only opposed alcohol usage but slavery as well, participating in the underground railroad.

8. Kreglinger, *Spirituality of Wine*, has a whole chapter on wine and alcohol abuse (180–98).

9. Capon, *Supper of the Lamb*, 85.

10. See for instance Howard-Brook, *Becoming Children of God*, 76–77.

11. Ehrenreich, *Dancing in the Streets*, 253. She explores this social dynamic throughout history, including church history and how clerical authorities kept the masses under

control by limiting their expressions of festive joy.

12. Brock and Parker, *Saving Paradise*, ix-xi.

13. Crossan, *Essential Jesus*, 13–20.

14. Brock and Parker, *Saving Paradise*, 224.

15. Stookey, *Eucharist*, 37.

16. Pollan, *Cooked*, 46, plays with this idea in relation to wines and cheeses.

17. Capon, *Party Spirit*, 12–14.

18. Streett, *Subversive Meals*, 140.

19. Resner, *Living In-Between*, 6–7.

20. The saying comes from the Babylonian Talmud and is cited in Scott, *Hear Then the Parable*, 356.

21. Moltmann, "Christianity," 11.

22. Resner, *Living In-Between*, 125.

23. I'm grateful to Valerie Bridgeman for these insights, and for her hosting me at the Methodist Theological Seminary in Ohio for lectures there. See Walker, *Hard Times Require Furious Dancing*.

24. Lewis, *Between Cross and Resurrection*.

25. For instance, see Smith, *Desiring the Kingdom*, 89–110.

26. Smith, *Symposium to Eucharist*, 136.

27. Ehrenreich, *Dancing in the Streets*, 137–41.

28. Cadwallader, *Anchoress*, 26, 100.

Chapter 4: The Conversation

1. A less embellished version of "the domestic goose" can be found in Kierkegaard, *Journals*, 252–53.

2. The "prompter" can be found in *Parables of Kierkegaard*, 89–90.

3. Clapp, *Peculiar People*, 115. See also, Ehrenreich, *Dancing in the Streets*, 210–11, who notes how one of the radical aspects of rock 'n' roll was audience participation besides just applauding at the end of a song. Similarly, when it comes to sports, she points out how compared to concert halls, stadiums are round. The crowds don't just see what's happening on the field among the teams but other parts of the crowd that incite people to enjoy games together (226–27).

4. Smith, *Symposium to Eucharist*, 28–29, 34–35.

5. A whole area of study in preaching theory (listener studies) has emerged in the last few years. Some of the more pertinent titles include: Allen, *Hearing the Sermon*; Allen Jr., *The Homiletic of All Believers*; and Powell, *What Do They Hear?*

6. Craddock, *As One Without Authority*, 46.

7. Kushner, *Nine Essential Things*, 3, 11.

8. While there are lots of sources about this, I am fond of the one by Cunningham, *These Three Are One*.

9. Smith, *Symposium to Eucharist*, 211.

10. Cox, *Future of Faith* , 26.

11. McClure, *Roundtable Pulpit*. See also his later work, *Other-Wise Preaching*.

12. One of the rare exceptions is Pagitt, *Preaching in the Inventive Age*. While I appreciate his endorsement of dialogical preaching, it's a shame his work isn't in conversation with other homiletical literature.

13. Lose, *Preaching at the Crossroads*.

14. Lose's three strategies include: 1) a more confessional than dogmatic (or "with certainty" approach since preachers clearly can't know anything with 100 percent certainty; 2) the use of more stories that show how sacred and secular are really one, especially when a sense of God's presence or transcendence is no longer obvious in our society; and 3) more dialogue, somewhat like the 2.0 version of the web online.

15. Cardenal, *Gospel in Solentiname*, xxiii.

16. Rice, *Embodied Word*.

17. McGowan, *Ancient Christian Worship*, 74.

18. Allen, Jr., *Homiletic of All Believers*, 45.

19. Boulton, *God Against Religion*, 64–93. Drawing on the writings of Karl Barth, Boulton goes on to suggest that although worship of God was not originally intended, God now chooses to redeem us through worship, to use that which humans have schemed for God's good purposes. While I find the initial diagnosis quite convincing, I'm not at all convinced of his conclusion.

20. Ibid., 185–86, also quotes these prophetic passages in a lengthy footnote, although he prefers to side with Barth in how they might be read more fruitfully than as outright critique of worship per se.

21. McGowan, *Ancient Christian Worship*, 5.

22. Banks, *Paul's Idea of Community*, 88–90. His discussion on the difference between the community formed in the first-century church as opposed to the "two fundamental institutions of ancient society: the family and the state" is fascinating (6–8, 190).

23. Aune, "Worship," 976. Lots of other scholars have suggested the same thing.

24. McGowan, *Ancient Christian Worship*, 66-67. See also Bradshaw, *Search for the Origins of Christian Worship*, 36–37.

25. Fox, *Spirituality Named Compassion*, 41–47. He contrasts the vertical dimensions of Jacob's ladder with Sarah's circle, although not always in terms of worship.

26. Butler Bass, *Grounded*, 11–12.

27. Volf, *Flourishing*, 202, 204, emphasis his.

28. Hall, *Confessing the Faith*, 101.

29. Packard and Hope, *Church Refugees*, 7, 31.

30. Ammerman, *Sacred Stories, Spiritual Tribes*, 302.

Conclusion: RSVP

1. Smith, *Symposium to Eucharist*, 21–25.

2. While I have called this an echo pattern, biblical scholars typically refer to it as a chiasm, named after the Greek letter Chi, which resembles an X. On this pattern in Luke 24, see Crossan, *Jesus*, 170–73.

3. Frederick Buechner plays with this image from Luke's story in a sermon in his collection, Buechner, *Magnificent Defeat*, 82–89. He preached a different sermon on this same passage in his collection of sermons, *Secrets in the Dark*, 251–57.

4. Frost and Hirsch, *Shaping of Things to Come*, 25.

5. Buechner, *Wishful Thinking*, 83.

6. Clapp, *Peculiar People*, 205.

7. Sweet, *From Tablet to Table*, 18.

8. Dillard, "Expedition," 38.

9. Ibid., 42.

10. Ibid., 58.

11. Marty, "From the Publisher," 3. Marty does not cite his source, and one wonders if he meant every Sunday rather than every day. But the numbers are alarming either way.

12. Butler Bass, *Grounded*, 19. Bass cites the per-year data from Zuckerman, *Living the Secular Life*, 60.

13. Hall, *Waiting for Gospel*, 25, claims that in Montreal, Canada, there are "more than fifty churches, many of them cathedral-sized," for sale.

14. Lathrop, "In Search," 5.

15. Tickle, *Great Emergence*, 16–17.

16. Marks, "Introduction," 1.

17. The quote is from Antoine de Saint-Exupéry and is cited in Fred Bahnson's wonderful memoir, *Soil and Sacrament*, 89.

Appendix: Different Words of Institution

1. Smith and Taussig, *Many Tables*, 113–35, have an entire closing chapter on different "eucharistic liturgies," with wonderful creative ideas, although no concrete suggestions in terms of different words of institution.

Bibliography

Allen, O. Wesley, Jr. *The Homiletic of All Believers: A Conversational Approach*. Louisville: Westminster John Knox, 2005.

Allen, Ronald J. *Hearing the Sermon: Relationship, Content, Feeling*. St. Louis: Chalice, 2004.

Ammerman, Nancy Tatom. *Sacred Stories, Spiritual Tribes: Finding Religion in Everyday Life*. Oxford: Oxford University Press, 2014.

Aune, David E. "Worship, Early Christian." In *Anchor Bible Dictionary*. New York: Doubleday, 1992.

Bahnson, Fred. *Soil and Sacrament: A Spiritual Memoir of Food and Faith*. New York: Simon and Schuster, 2013.

Banks, Robert J. *Paul's Idea of Community: The Early House Churches in Their Cultural Setting*. Rev. ed. Grand Rapids: Baker Academic, 2012.

Barth, Markus. *Rediscovering the Lord's Supper: Communion with Israel, with Christ, and Among the Guests*. Atlanta: John Knox, 1988.

Berry, Wendell. *Jayber Crow*. Washington, DC: Counterpoint, 2000.

Boin, Douglas. *Coming Out Christian in the Roman World: How the Followers of Jesus Made a Place in Caesar's Empire*. New York: Bloomsbury, 2015.

Boulton, Matthew Myer. *God Against Religion: Rethinking Christian Theology through Worship*. Grand Rapids: Eerdmans, 2008.

Bradshaw, Paul F. *The Search for the Origins of Christian Worship: Sources and Methods for the Study of Early Liturgy*. 2nd ed. Oxford: Oxford University Press, 2002.

Brock, Rita Nakashima, and Rebecca Ann Parker. *Saving Paradise: How Christianity Traded Love of This World for Crucifixion and Empire*. Boston: Beacon, 2008.

Buechner, Frederick. *The Magnificent Defeat*. San Francisco: Harper and Row, 1966.

———. *Secrets in the Dark: A Life in Sermons*. New York: HarperSanFrancisco, 2006.

———. *Wishful Thinking: A Theological ABC*. New York: Harper and Row, 1973.

Butler Bass, Diana. *Grounded: Finding God in the Word: A Spiritual Revolution*. New York: HarperOne, 2015.

Cadwallader, Robyn. *The Anchoress*. New York: Sarah Crichton, 2015.

Capon, Robert Farrar. *The Supper of the Lamb: A Culinary Reflection*. Garden City, NY: Doubleday, 1969.

———. *Party Spirit: Some Entertaining Principles*. New York: William Morrow, 1979.

Cardenal, Ernesto. *The Gospel in Solentiname*. Translated by Donald D. Walsh. Maryknoll, NY: Orbis, 2010.

Clapp, Rodney. *A Peculiar People: The Church as Culture in a Post-Christian Society.* Downers Grove, IL: IVP Academic, 1996.

Corley, Kathleen. *Private Women, Public Meals: Social Conflict in the Synoptic Tradition.* Peabody, MA: Hendrickson, 1993.

Cox, Harvey. *The Future of Faith.* New York: HarperOne, 2009.

Craddock, Fred B. *Craddock Stories.* Edited by Mike Graves and Richard F. Ward. St. Louis: Chalice, 2001.

———. *As One Without Authority.* Rev. ed. St. Louis: Chalice, 2001.

Crossan, John Dominic. *The Birth of Christianity: Discovering What Happened in the Years Immediately after the Execution of Jesus.* New York: HarperSanFrancisco, 1998.

———. *The Essential Jesus: Original Sayings and Earliest Images.* Edison, NJ: Castle, 1998.

———. *The Greatest Prayer: Rediscovering the Revolutionary Message of the Lord's Prayer.* New York: HarperOne, 2010.

———. *Jesus: A Revolutionary Biography.* New York: HarperSanFrancisco, 1994.

Cunningham, David S. *These Three Are One: The Practice of Trinitarian Theology.* Malden, MA: Blackwell, 1998.

Dillard, Annie. "An Expedition to the Pole." In *Teaching a Stone to Talk: Expeditions and Encounters,* 35–70. New York: HarperPerennial, 1982.

———. *For the Time Being.* New York: Alfred A. Knopf, 1999.

———. *Holy the Firm.* New York: HarperPerennial, 1977.

Ehrenreich, Barbara. *Dancing in the Streets: A History of Collective Joy.* New York: Picador, 2006.

Fowler, Robert M. *Let the Reader Understand: Reader Response Criticism and the Gospel of Mark.* Harrisburg, PA: Trinity, 1996.

Fox, Matthew. *A Spirituality Named Compassion and the Healing of the Global Village, Humpty Dumpty and Us.* New York: Harper and Row, 1990.

Frost, Michael, and Alan Hirsch. *The Shaping of Things to Come: Innovation and Mission of the 21st Century.* Rev. ed. Grand Rapids: Baker, 2013.

Gopnik, Adam. *The Table Comes First: Family, France, and the Meaning of Food.* New York: Vintage, 2011.

Greeley, Andrew. *The Catholic Imagination.* Berkeley, CA: The University of California Press, 2000.

Hall, Douglas John. *Confessing the Faith: Christian Theology in a North American Context.* Minneapolis: Fortress, 1996.

———. *Waiting for Gospel: An Appeal to the Dispirited Remnants of Protestant "Establishment."* Eugene, OR: Cascade, 2012.

Honoré, Carl. *In Praise of Slowness: Challenging the Cult of Speed.* New York: HarperSanFrancisco, 2004.

Howard-Brook, Wes. *Becoming Children of God: John's Gospel and Radical Discipleship.* Maryknoll, NY: Orbis, 1994.

Howard Merritt, Carol. "Leading Like Lydia." *The Christian Century,* March 2, 2016, 45.

James, William. *The Varieties of Religious Experience: A Study in Human Nature.* New York: Modern Library, 1902.

Julier, Alice P. *Eating Together: Food, Friendship, and Inequality.* Urbana, IL: University of Illinois Press, 2013.

Karris, Robert J. *Eating Your Way through Luke's Gospel.* Collegeville, MN: Order of Saint Benedict, 2006.

Kierkegaard, Søren. *Journals*. Edited and translated by Alexander Dru. New York: Harper Torchbooks, 1959.

———. *Parables of Kierkegaard*. Edited by Thomas C. Oden. Princeton, NJ: Princeton University Press, 1978.

Klinghardt, Matthias. *Gemeinschaftsmahl und Mahlgemeinschaft: Soziologie und Liturgie fruhchristlicher Mahlfeiern*. Tubingen: Francke Verlag, 1996.

Kreglinger, Gisela H. *The Spirituality of Wine*. Grand Rapids: Eerdmans, 2016.

Kushner, Harold S. *Nine Essential Things I've Learned about Life*. New York: Alfred A. Knopf, 2015.

Lathrop, Chuck. "In Search of a Roundtable." In *A Gentle Presence*, 5. Washington, DC: Appalachian Documentation, 1977.

Lathrop, Gordon W. *The Four Gospels on Sunday: The New Testament and the Reform of Christian Worship*. Minneapolis: Fortress, 2012.

Levine, Amy-Jill. *The Misunderstood Jew: The Church and the Scandal of the Jewish Jesus*. New York: HarperOne, 2006.

Lewis, Alan E. *Between Cross and Resurrection: A Theology of Holy Saturday*. Grand Rapids: Eerdmans, 2001.

Lose, David J. *Preaching at the Crossroads: How the World—and Our Preaching—Is Changing*. Minneapolis: Fortress, 2013.

Marks, Susan. "Introduction." In *Meals in Early Judaism: Social Formation at the Table*, edited by Susan Marks and Hal Taussig, 1–12. New York: Palgrave Macmillan, 2014.

Marty, Peter W. "From the Publisher." *The Christian Century*. August 31, 2016, 3.

McClure, John S. *Other-Wise Preaching: A Postmodern Ethic for Homiletics*. St. Louis: Chalice, 2001.

———. *The Roundtable Pulpit: Where Leadership and Preaching Meet*. Nashville: Abingdon, 1995.

McGowan, Andrew B. *Ancient Christian Worship: Early Church Practices in Social, Historical, and Theological Perspective*. Grand Rapids: Baker Academic, 2014.

Meeks, Wayne A. *The First Urban Christians: The Social World of the Apostle Paul*. 2nd ed. Hew Haven, CT: Yale University Press, 2003.

Merritt, Carol Howard. "Leading Like Lydia." *The Christian Century*. March 2, 1016, 45.

Miles, Sara. *Take This Bread: The Spiritual Memoir of a Twenty-First Century Christian*. New York: Ballantine, 2008.

Moltmann, Jürgen. "Christianity: A Religion of Joy." In *Joy and Human Flourishing: Essays on Theology, Culture, and the Good Life*, edited by Miroslav Volf and Justin E. Crisp, 1–15. Minneapolis: Fortress, 2015.

Neusner, Jacob, and Bruce Chilton, eds. *In Quest of the Historical Pharisees*. Waco, TX: Baylor University Press, 2007.

Newman, John Henry. *An Essay on the Development of Christian Doctrine*. Garden City, NY: Image, 1960.

Niequist, Shauna. *Bread and Wine: A Love Letter to Life Lived Around the Table with Recipes*. Grand Rapids: Zondervan, 2013.

Norris, Kathleen. *The Quotidian Mysteries: Laundry, Liturgy and "Women's Work."* New York: Paulist, 1998.

Packard, Josh, and Ashleigh Hope. *Church Refugees: Sociologists Reveal Why People Are Done with Church but Not Their Faith*. Loveland, CO: Group, 2015.

Packer, James. "Housing and Population in Imperial Ostia and Rome." *Journal of Roman Studies* 57 (1967) 80–95.

————. *The Insulae of Imperial Ostia*. Rome: American Academy of Rome, 1971.

Pagitt, Doug. *Preaching in the Inventive Age*. Nashville: Abingdon, 2014.

Pervo, Richard. *Profit with Delight: The Literary Genre of the Acts of the Apostles*. Minneapolis: Fortress, 1987.

Pollan, Michael. *Cooked: A Natural History of Transformation*. New York: Penguin, 2013.

Powell, Mark Allan. *What Do They Hear? Bridging the Gap Between Pulpit and Pew*. Nashville: Abingdon, 2007.

Resner, André. *Living In-Between: Lament, Justice, and the Persistence of the Gospel*. Eugene, OR: Cascade, 2015.

Rice, Charles L. *The Embodied Word: Preaching as Art and Liturgy*. Minneapolis: Fortress, 1991.

Schlosser, Eric. *Fast Food Nation: The Dark Side of the All-American Meal*. Boston: Mariner, 2012.

Schmemann, Alexander. *For the Life of the World: Sacraments and Orthodoxy*. Crestwood, NY: St.Valdimir's Seminary Press, 1973.

Scott, Bernard Brandon. *Hear Then the Parable: A Commentary on the Parables of Jesus*. Minneapolis: Fortress, 1989.

Shelton, Jo-Ann. *As the Romans Did: A Source Book in Roman Social History*. New York: Oxford University Press, 1988.

Smith, C. Christopher, and John Pattison. *Slow Church: Cultivating Community in the Patient Way of Jesus*. Downers Grove, IL: Intervarsity, 2014.

Smith, Dennis E. *From Symposium to Eucharist: The Banquet in the Early Christian World*. Minneapolis: Fortress, 2003.

Smith, Dennis E., and Hal E. Taussig. *Many Tables: The Eucharist in the New Testament and Liturgy Today*. Eugene, OR: Wipf and Stock, 2001.

Smith, James K. A. *Desiring the Kingdom: Worship, Worldview, and Cultural Formation*. Grand Rapids: Baker Academic, 2009.

Standhartinger, Angela. "Women in Early Christian Meal Gatherings: Discourse and Reality" In *Meals in the Early Christian World: Social Formation, Experimentation, and Conflict at the Table*, edited by Dennis E. Smith and Hal E. Taussig, 87–108. New York: Palgrave Macmillan, 2012.

Stookey, Laurence Hull. *Eucharist: Christ's Feast with the Church*. Nashville: Abingdon, 1993.

Streett, R. Alan. *Subversive Meals: An Analysis of the Lord's Supper under Roman Domination during the First Century*. Eugene, OR: Pickwick, 2013.

Suttle, Tim. *Shrink: Faithful Ministry in a Church-Growth Culture*. Grand Rapids: Zondervan, 2014,

Sweet, Leonard. *From Tablet to Table: Where Community Is Found and Identity Is Formed*. Colorado Springs: NavPress, 2014.

Tickle, Phyllis. *The Great Emergence: How Christianity Is Changing and Why*. Grand Rapids: Baker, 2008.

Volf, Miroslav. *Flourishing: Why We Need Religion in a Globalized World*. New Haven, CT: Yale University Press, 2017.

Walker, Alice. *Hard Times Require Furious Dancing*. Novato, CA: New World Library, 2010.

Wirzba, Norman. *Food and Faith: A Theology of Eating*. Cambridge: Cambridge University Press, 2011.

Witherington, Ben, III. *Making a Meal of It: Rethinking the Theology of the Lord's Supper.* Waco, TX: Baylor University Press, 2008.

Wright, N. T. "Joy: Some New Testament Perspectives and Questions." In *Joy and Human Flourishing: Essays on Theology, Culture, and the Good Life,* edited by Miroslav Volf and Justin E. Crisp, 39–61. Minneapolis: Fortress, 2015.

Zuckerman, Phil. *Living the Secular Life.* New York: Penguin, 2014.